FROM PENNILESS TO PUBLISHER

Sell Your Books From Prison:

TRICKS, TACTICS AND SECRETS FROM A <u>PRO</u>

* LEARN WHY MARKETING BEGINS BEFORE THE FIRST CHAPTER.

* ACCESS A MILLION POTENTIAL READERS IN 30 MINUTES.

* DISCOVER HOW TO IDENTIFY, REACH AND CONVERT READERS TO BUYERS.

* WHAT SELLS BOOKS, WHEN BOOKS SELL AND WHY?

$24.98

GEORGE KAYER AND VINNIE VALE

WHAT OUR CUSTOMERS SAY

Great job on the ad and analytics, I would have never thought to engage in Europe.
Silence in the Face of Injustice by Gary Hardy Ph.D.

I feel like the Beta Test is a cool system. Thank you for your teamwork and service.
Penitentiary Workout by Ghetto Chef.

Thank you so much for all you and Ken do, I am grateful.
Art by Clinton Airheart by Clinton Airheart

Thank you as always for corresponding. That's why I tell people y'all are the best! I love the communication.
100 Ways to Make Money in Prison by Baby Auk

Peace to Cadmus, keep up the good work.
Urban Drip Magazine by Don Reynolds.

All I can say is WOW! It's like this cover was waiting for my book. It couldn't be more perfect.
A Pastor's Profession by Gerald Thomas.

George, what you have done from prison is beyond amazing. Cadmus authors are fortunate to have you guiding their publishing journey.
Inmate Shopper by Freebird Publishers.

Thanks for doubling my sales. You're the real deal.
Writing For Their Lives by Roger Murray.

WHAT OUR CUSTOMERS SAY

I'm super excited that you are willing to help us get our music out there for people to hear.
Shattered Souls band by Dylan,

Thank you immensely for your insights on my manuscript.
Psymple Nvestor by Paul Lee.

I really appreciate your enthusiasm. Continue to be great.
H.O.P.E. by Brittany Monk

Thanks for the newsletter and letting me know what was going on. I thought the EFT was a scam.
N.B.U. by Pepi McKenzie

Thanks for taking Care of business, I contacted the BBB and let them know the issue is resolved.
A Light of Other Suns by Angelo Niles

Excellent!!! A great (marketing) idea.
Life Without A Period by Kevin Schaddenmire

I feel blessed to be working with you and your staff for my children's books.
Cornell Shawell.

Mr. George, you telling me you accepted my children's book manuscript for publication blew my mind. I'm so excited, in tears excited. Thank you.
Built For Greatness by Monique Houston.

I'm glad you guys bought Cadmus and reformed it for the better.
Living in Reality by David Jones

SELL YOUR BOOKS FROM PRISON:
Tips, Tactics, and Secrets From A Pro

George Kayer

and Vinnie Vale

Cadmus Publishing
CadmusPublishing.com

SELL YOUR BOOKS FROM PRISON:
Tips, Tactics, and Secrets From A Pro

Manufactured in the United States of America. Copyright 2024 by George R. Kayer and Vinnie Vale. All rights reserved. No part of this book may be reproduced in any form, audio, digital, or in print, except excerpts by reviewers, without written permission from the copyright holder or Cadmus Publishing LLC.

Published by Cadmus Publishing LLC. P. O. Box 8664. Haledon, NJ 07538
Phone: 360.565.6459
Web: Cadmuspublishing.com
Web: BooksByPrisoners.com
Web: MusicbyPrisoners.com
Facebook.com/Cadmuspublishing
Business email: admin@cadmuspublishing.com
Author email: info@cadmuspublishing.com

ISBN# 978-1-63751-475-7
Library of Congress Control Number: 2024938497
Book catalog info. Categories.
  Business and Economics/Marketing
Computers/Desktop Publishing

Cadmus Publishing
CadmusPublishing.com

TABLE OF CONTENTS:

THE FISH -- PART ONE.

1. Do I Have To Learn Marketing, I'm A Writer?......................1

2. Why We Are The Cats To School Ya Up On Marketing Your Books...4

3.. Getting A Grip On The Publishing Hood..............................7

4. When Should I Begin Thinking About Marketing?...............12

5. Who Are You Writing For?...15

6. Pulling Your Own Weight..18

7. Write A Book In 30 Days? Yo, Step Off!...............................20

THE CONVICT -- PART TWO.

8. The Secret Sauce: Editing..22

9. The Power Of The Query Letter...26

10. Taking Your Ms For A Joy Ride..29

11. Getting Your Book Cover Slung Down..............................31

12. Title? Oh My Title, Where Art Thou?..................................38

13. The Layouts...45

THE SHOT CALLER: PART THREE

14. All About The Benjamin's Baby? Maybe Not.......................47

15. Why Doesn't My Book Sell: Metada................................49

16. The Science Of Getting A Book Noticed..........................52
*** Pen Pimping?
*** Word Of Mouth, Ain't What It Use To Be, Or Is It?
*** Who Doesn't Enjoy A Damn Good Article?

17. Small Budget Advertising..59

18. Affordable Alternatives To An Ad Campaign....................62

19. Social Media = Social Money..65

20. The Slow Lonesome Death Of Print Ads.........................68

21. So You Want An Author's Website?................................70

22. Book Reviewers, Blurbs, Book Bloggers.........................77

23. Press Release? Why Should I Care?..79

24. Brick And Mortar Bookstores...83

25. Keeping A Stash Of Books..85

26. Why Should I Write Another Book? Momentum!....................87

27. Writing From Prison And The Law..90

Afterword...92

Glossary..94

Services offered by cadmus...103

Tips for correcting your ms draft. (A cad doc)

Frequently Asked Questions FAQs..111

Publications who publish prisoners...122

SELL YOUR BOOKS FROM PRISON

Legal disclaimer

This book is intended for informational purposes only. The contents herein are not intended to provide legal, financial, or any other professional advice. The author and publisher make no representations or warranties of any kind with respect to the accuracy, applicability, fitness, or completeness of the contents of this book.

The information contained in this book is based on the author's understanding of the topic at the time of writing and is subject to change. The author and publisher shall not be held liable for any errors, omissions, or any outcomes related to the use of this information.

Readers are advised to seek professional advice tailored to their specific circumstances before making any decisions or taking any actions based on the information contained in this book. The author and publisher disclaim any liability, loss, or risk incurred as a consequence, directly or indirectly, of the use and application of any of the contents of this book.

Any reference to specific individuals, companies, products, or services is for illustrative purposes only and does not constitute an endorsement or recommendation by the author or publisher.

And any other trademarks, service marks, product names, or named features mentioned in this book are the property of their respective owners and are used solely for the purpose of identifying the specific entities, events, or products described in this book.

The views and opinions expressed in this book are those of the author and do not necessarily reflect the official policy or position of any other agency, organization, employer, or company.

By reading this book, you agree to indemnify, defend, and hold harmless the author and publisher from and against any and all claims, damages, losses, liabilities, and expenses (including but not limited to attorneys' fees) arising from your use of the information provided in this book.

GEORGE R. KAYER AND VINNIE VALE

THE FISH -- PART ONE.

Chapter 1

DO I HAVE TO LEARN MARKETING, I'M A WRITER ?

The short answer is "Yes". The long answer is "Yes". PEOPLE CANT BUY YOUR BOOK IF THEY DONT KNOW ABOUT IT! Unless you have $10,000 to $50,000 to hire a marketing company, your gonna need to learn the ins and outs of the marketing game. Its gonna be up to you and the choices you make regarding your book that determines whether its successful or not. And in the end, success comes down to marketing.

If you're still going to the chow hall everyday, and not eating out of the store or burger shack, then you need to read this book. That means if you wanna sell books, you gotta have the schooling. The long answer is still "Yes," just with a lot more lingo.

It was ran down to you in the Intro, right about in the middle, so we hope you read it, **people can't buy your book if they don't know about it.** That one line is golden, so let's try it again, with gusto

Check it out, its simple. It seems that too many of y'all trying to make it in this game forget that basic fact. Authors say: "We'll, my shits on Amazon. When people are scanning through my books genre, they'll find it!" Or maybe they say, "I got me an author page, and I can get on a cell phone and mess around with social media, so when peeps see that, they'll find my shit from there." Seeing and buying are two different birds.

Negative ghost rider, that bird don't fly. There are millions of books out there, and likely hundreds or thousands of books in your genre alone, for real. Odds of peeps just stumbling onto your shit are slim to none. The same goes for any website, or whatever social media you've been able to scrounge together.

That's not saying you should just call it quits, or even skip over having a social media presence/website - those are both excellent assets which we will run down to you later.

But you need that extra oomph, ya dig? And you do have options, even in the joint. Your options will vary widely based on your budget and the network available to you - both in peeps and in dollar signs. Some shits cheap or free, but need peeps to put the work in for you. Some take a bank roll but require less personal time, or at least are easily hired out. If your budget is lazy but you're dedicated, we can help you navigate the book part. But if you are lazy, you may as well stop reading now. Or if you have too many other priorities than dedicated time for marketing.

This is where many peeps in the free world get into the proverbial train wreck: they work 9 to 5's, they deal with family and social lives, daily dramas, and anything else you can think of. As most of us unfortunately know, even with a steady legal income most folks are living hand to mouth, and they damn sure ain't got the money to fund pet projects or your project.

As you can probably see - you've already got one ace in the hole that those on the streets don't have: YOU GOT ALL THE TIME IN THE WORLD PLAYER! Its true that many of us have them bogus $0.50 prison jobs, and they can take up some of our free time, and like most convicts, I'm sure you love chilling on the yard politicking with your homeboys, and maybe you even got a side hustle going to make a little extra pocket change. But real talk, we don't need to worry about a crib, grub, or fresh duds. We can cut back on our socializing. There are many ways for us to find significantly more free time than folks on the streets. So find it, and fuckin use it! You don't have much in the way of prospects where you are, but TIME you do have! Use that shit wisely. Now, if you have the bank roll or loved ones lookin' out for you, or maybe you even got some peoples from your neighborhood that can be convinced to invest in you and your book, then your in the right spot to make a dent in the literary world. So get it done.

Marketing is not a one time thing, either. Word of mouth don't work in this industry. Think about Coca Cola. You know what Coca Cola is right? In fact, do you know anyone that doesn't know what Coca Cola is? Yet you still see their adds on TV, in magazines, or hear them on the radio. Why's that you think? Why do they spend tens of millions of dollars a year on advertising, are they just stupid? Do you think there are people out there who still don't know about Coca Cola?

The fact is no, they are not stupid. In fact their geniuses. Let me tell you why: Repetition. Repetition vs Right place Right time. If shit ain't in your head at the right time, the right moment... you'll forget about it, when you could be buying it. Repetition is key to successful marketing. In outlaw terms, think about sometimes when you re-up your sack.. you give out free $20 bags every once in awhile, let everybody get a taste so their teeth start ringing. That's repetitive marketing player. Those big brands like Coca Cola already know about repetitive marketing. And now, so do you. Your welcome.

Anyways, well get into more about marketing and repetition later. That was all said to say this: Yes, you really need to market your book!... Long answer.

Chapter 2

"WHO THE HELL ARE WE TO TELL YOU HOW TO MARKET YOUR BOOK?"

Good question, but let me ask you this: Do you know how to market a book? That's what I thought. But fear not, because we truly do have the background to provide you with the 411 on marketing. First, we literally wrote THE book on marketing from the joint (which should be obvious, cause you're reading it right now). On the real, if you read the back cover you read about my coauthor George, one of the most published prisoners in America.

On top of that, just like you we also have the misfortune of currently being in the joint, and have published books from here. Geo has also worked with 100's of incarcerated authors who were not only on yards with him, but also in other prison units across the U.S. He has seen the legit work that comes out of prisons, and he has also seen more times than he can count how it falls dead in the dirt by not reaching the audience it deserves simply cause the author didn't know the science behind the marketing game. Now, there are a grip of marketing books out there, and we recommend a handful of em. But very few of them are written by a convict, targeted specifically to other convicts (see Appendix A for some good suggestions).

Peeps on the streets can go online and find a grip of resources, tips, recommendations, and a whole slew of other info on how to market their book. They can also pay consultants and companies to do the marketing for them. They don't need a shit ton of books telling them the same things in different ways. But we convicts only have books. And our cell space is limited, so we don't need a whole shelf of books explaining the same shit over and over again. Unfortunately, there aren't to many aimed directly towards us. This is distressing to Geo and I cause there should be a lot more bestsellers amongst the prison populations.

Why is that you ask? Cause who else has such great opportunities to get their career off the ground? And there's just something about the stories and experiences that we convicts have accumulated throughout or lives that sets us apart from the legal side of society. Sadly, there are convicts out there who have written upwards of Fifty books, but could not figure out how to get them out to the world. There have been far to many books that either not get published at all, or take a shit in sales because the convicts didn't have the resources or knowledge to make it happen.

But anyways, as I was saying, Geo has worked with the convict population of society a lot throughout his 14 year career. Shit, I'm doing what I'm doing today because of him. We both know the restrictions and hurdles you face, cause we face them to we also know the resources you may have to overcome the hurdles put in your way, cause once again, we too have used said resources to leap over those hurdles.

We have made it our goal in life to see as many convict authors succeed and make a career in this game.

So too has this become the goal of Cadmus Publishing (the very publishers who are releasing this book). They have really stepped up to the plate in their support of convict authors. Most importantly, they work directly with convict authors: accepting phone calls, snail mail, and many prison email systems. That alone sets them apart from most other publishing houses out there. Freebird Publishers has stopped using prisoner email and CellBlock is no longer accepting publishing gigs

There are a few books out there - written by convicts - that school you on how to write a book from the joint. How to get it published. What worked for them. What didn't work. Many of these books keep it one hundred: we've read dozens of em over the years.

However, most of em are geared towards writing and publishing urban novels. Some have a couple marketing tips. Some have really good advice. A1 excellent advice, we would go as far to say. But they fall short on turning you book into fat stacks. Some have only one or two ideas. Some require a large, helpful network of peeps on the outside. Some are geared to only one type of book.

    This book right here is our gift to you. Written by convicts for convicts. In it we fill in the gaps left by those other books - the general marketing books. As I write this, I assume you've written a great book. YOU know you've written a great book or maybe your ready to do so - and big ups for getting and reading this book before you start!
    I assume all of this cause this book is here to help you get rich from Your book. Geo and I are going to share with you - as a convict author - what options you have for getting your shit into as many hands as possible and start bringing in the bank. Its time to max out your store limit every week. Its time for you to make all the calls you want. Its time for YOU to send money home to your family for a change. You can make a truck load of cash with the right book from where you sit. And we've got the experience, skills, and knowledge to get you there. The material in this book is golden. These options WORK. We've made them work for ourselves. We've seen them work for others. We've even heard of convicts taking their books to their parole hearings, or to their judge, along with the royalty statements, proving they can make it on the outside without resorting back to criminal enterprises.

    It don't matter what your in for. It don't matter if your a dude or a chick. It don't matter how long you're down for - or if you've been laid down with a life sentence. What matters is that you got a story to tell, and it deserves to be told, and let me tell you, peeps are gonna love it. You got this. From right where you stand.   Ten
                Toes
                Down.

Chapter 3

"GETTING THE GRIP ON THE PUBLISHING HOOD"

Navigating the Publishing Landscape: Traditional, Hybrid, and Self-Publishing Services

The landscape of the publishing industry has undergone significant transformations in recent years, offering authors diverse paths to bring their literary creations to the world. Traditional publishers, hybrid publishers, and self-publishing services companies each have distinct characteristics, benefits, and drawbacks. In this article, we'll delve into the differences between these publishing models, exploring royalty agreements, promotional efforts, and the elusive world of cash advances.

Traditional Publishers:

Traditional publishing like Cadmus Publishing have long been the bastion of the literary world. Authors who secure contracts with traditional publishers often benefit from a cash advance against future royalties, providing financial support during the writing process. However, these advances are typically reserved for well-known or celebrity writers with proven market appeal.

Royalty agreements in traditional publishing vary but usually hover around 8-15% of the book's cover price. While this model offers the prestige of being associated with established publishing houses, there are drawbacks. Traditional publishers often allocate a relatively small budget for book promotion, leaving authors to fend for themselves in the highly competitive market. Additionally, promotional chargebacks—deductions from an author's royalties to cover marketing expenses—can be a bitter pill to swallow.

Hybrid Publishers:

Hybrid publishing like Cadmus represents a middle ground between traditional and self-publishing models. These publishers combine elements of both, providing authors with greater creative control while offering professional editing, design, and distribution services for a fee. One of the standout features of hybrid publishing is the more favorable royalty agreements compared to traditional publishers.

Hybrid publishers typically offer royalties ranging from ranging from 20% to 40% of cover price for free people and 20% to 25% for people in prisons who do not have bank accounts and are unable to manage their own distribution. Authors may purchase Author copies for resale and increase their profits too. This gives authors a more substantial share of the earnings from their book sales. This increased financial incentive aligns the interests of the author and the publisher more closely. Additionally, hybrid publishers may provide some promotional support, although the extent varies widely. Authors still need to take an active role in marketing their work, but the increased royalties can be a powerful motivator.

Self-Publishing Services Companies:

Self-publishing has surged in popularity due to its accessibility and the democratization of the publishing process. Self-publishing services companies empower authors to take control of their projects, from writing to distribution. However, it's crucial for authors to understand that promotion is primarily their responsibility in the self-publishing realm.

Self-publishing platforms typically charge authors for various services, such as editing, cover design, and distribution. While this model allows for greater creative freedom, it places the onus on authors to invest in their book's success. The advantage lies in the potential for higher royalties, often exceeding 70% of the cover price when buying 100 or more books at a time. Yet, without the marketing machinery of traditional or hybrid publishers, authors must navigate the intricacies of book promotion independently.

Conclusion:

Choosing the right publishing path depends on an author's goals, resources, and preferences. Traditional publishers offer prestige and, for some, the allure of a cash advance, but they often allocate minimal resources for book promotion. Hybrid publishers strike a balance, providing authors with higher royalties and some promotional support. Meanwhile, self-publishing services companies grant unparalleled creative control but require authors to spearhead their marketing efforts.

In this dynamic publishing landscape, understanding the nuances of each model is crucial. Authors must weigh the benefits and drawbacks to make an informed decision that aligns with their objectives. Whether seeking the validation of a traditional publisher, the flexibility of a hybrid model, or the autonomy of self-publishing, authors can now chart their own course in the literary world.

Its said that: "50% of all marketing works. But no one knows which 50%".
So what the hell is marketing? Well, you can break it down into 3 discrete styles:
PUBLICITY: This is anything that draws attention to you as the author, or to your book. If you appear in the news for any reason, that can be viewed as publicity. Doing a radio interview? That's publicity. Did some peeps write any articles about you? Publicity. Basically if you didn't dole out cash for it directly, that's publicity. That's the meaning of, "there's no such thing as bad publicity".
PROMOTION: Any kinda swag that promotes your book,

from bookmarks to posters, hoodies with your cover art.

ADVERTISING: Anytime YOU spend divets to advertise your shit in books, magazines, or on the internet.

That's the basic roll call for the definitions and a simplified way to categorize different types of marketing. Some ideas in this book will get the grip on a couple of these categories. Some ideas might be a bitch to squeeze into any one category and will have a greasy feel from anything else. But keeping these concepts in the mental can help you come up with your own steelo, and also help keep your head on straight as you read up on the concepts and ideas we're gonna be running down to you.

A big question we hear a lot is, "how much money can I expect to make from my book?" The answer is... Nobody really knows that science. There are Beta test ad campaigns that can tell if digital ads will generate enough sales to make money. The shit that will dictate how successful a book will be are so widely varied, so impossible to get the science on, and so completely unpredictable, that there ain't a cat in this industry who can say with any facts which book will succeed and which will take a shit. This is why big named authors have had their shit rejected from major publishers dozens of times before their names finally started ringing bells. Steven King, for example, submitted his first books dozens of times before a publisher gave him the time of day. You may have heard of Inmate Shopper, one of Geo's books before he sold it to Freebird. He offered it to 24 publishers, Nada. So he self published, and it is still, 12 years later the #1 selling prisoner resource book. The Harry Potter books were shot down by 12 major publishers before getting a nod. (One has to assume some cat got canned over that oops!) But this same whacked out shit is also why some books that get called up to play in the majors fail miserably, even at breaking even. There's just no science on how to determine success.

But check game, as we've said - No one can buy your shit if they don't know it exists (has this mantra made it through your skull yet?). That's where we are now - now one knows your shit exists. This is why you need to read this, cover to cover, and then read it over again a few more times. Get this schooling ingrained in you as if they were yard politics, and you need to know them to survive.. then start doing SOMETHING. Pick and choose what game plans will work for you. And don't get pissy if your title don't generate an immediate rush of sales.

Geo here, I took my last coin and ran an ad in Prison Legal News, sure that all I needed was a shot in that mag. I received four sales that month. I was wrecked. I knew I had a winner, why didn't people buy??

Keep reading.

Sometimes it takes a little time to really break into your stride. Sometimes it takes a lot of failures before you can succeed. The key is to keep trying. Be an energetic pitbull in a dog fight.

We're going to be referencing a lot of resources in this here book. We can't cover all of them in here and for many of you it ain't gonna matter - most are found online, or may not accept convict clients (I.E haters), etc. No sweat, Cadmus got ya covered.

Shit like how to use software to find the best keywords by following some specific methods on the internet. Again, Cadmus got ya. There's a lot of hella complex things that can be done by peeps who have full access to the internet and other resources on the streets. However, this book ain't for them. There are plenty of Tiktok videos that will school them on that.

Finally, READ THIS ENTIRE BOOK. Even sections you think are bogus and not relevant to you. There may be a golden goose egg of useful information in there that is Very relevant to you, even though the rest of the section may not be. Plus, reading all this shit may lead to some badass ideas of your own. If its one thing we've learned, we convicts can be very resourceful and come up with shit others may not have realized would be possible. Become the prison MacGyver of convict publishing.

… GEORGE R. KAYER AND VINNIE VALE

Chapter 4

"WHEN SHOULD I THINK ABOUT MARKETING?

The time you should begin to think about marketing is from the very start. Split your mind into two halves, one half dedicated to the concept and creation of your book, and the other half dedicated to how your going to present this book to society. Think about who's gonna wanna read that book, and how your going bring their attention to it. Here in AZ we have a podcast app on our tablets. It offers a wide range of podcasts that cover various topics. We here in AZ could therefore make a list of podcasts that we could submit our book to for their consideration of review and/or advertisement. This is just one example that you could be contemplating while writing your book. Even if you've already written your book, you can work on figuring out what avenues your already aware of that your book can be marketed through. The actual process of marketing doesn't begin until your book is nearly ready for print, or already published.

Before you even begin to get your book ready for publishing, it needs value. Meaning it needs an original concept, or an updated/new view point on an already existing concept. Then it needs to be well written, and entertaining. Something that keeps the reader engrossed in what your saying, regardless if its fiction or nonfiction. If its fiction, then things like twists that catch the reader off guard are important. If its nonfiction, it will need information that most readers haven't experienced in the topic before, or it needs some type of "revelation" type info that the reader can apply their lives. Doing these things causes a word-of-mouth scenario to take place. You want as many people as possible to recommend your book to everyone they know. I'm gonna let Geo take over for a little bit, so that he can give you a quick master class in pre-publishing fundamentals.

   Geo here,
   It is such a pleasure to work with Vinnie on this project. Often, working with a coauthor can suck, and has nearly caused many marital divorces. No, we aren't a couple so don't go there. See, you are able to benefit from both our point of views and experiences in this crazy business. What Vinnie brings to us is a naivete point of view from a new writer, stumbling through exactly what you may be experiencing, stuff I honestly have nearly forgotten about. The foundational stuff I learned long ago that is just automatic to me now. By us bouncing these how to concepts and practices of the pages I can catch statements he makes and adjust or elaborate on them. Here's a perfect example:
   In the previous paragraph Vinnie wrote:

   The actual process of marketing doesn't begin until your book is nearly ready for print, or already published.
   Now I could have simply edited that out because previously he covered the importance of thinking about marketing while you are writing your book. But now comes my point of view, that of an editor and publisher. This question of "who will read what I'm writing" is so critical that it is the First question an editor of a magazine or blog ask when considering reviewing or writing an article about your book. If you're going to submit your book to Penguin or Random House or me for traditional publishing, we ask a similar question: who will buy this book? We will read your query and if you didn't clearly and exactly identify who will read and buy your book, we may not even read the first chapter of your manuscript. If anyone is to be a successful cook or driver one must learn the basics of those skills. It's the same with writing.

   Believe me when I tell you, editors and publishers, we spend all our time searching for you, if you know the basics. Your ego is your worse enemy. Your ego tells you: my book is the next New York Times Best Seller, I don't have to fill out no stupid ass query, they're lucky I'm giving them a chance to publish my book. The reality is your book may be a Best Seller but if you don't prepare an exciting, detailed query for us to look at, we will probably never read your manuscript.

My ego use to tell me the same shit so I know this from experience. And now that I've been an editor of several periodicals and a now a publisher with 600 authors under our roof I understand why editors and publishers toss out the majority of queries and manuscripts. Its so simple, time. It's not us being elitist egomaniacs, it's time.

If I have to choose between looking at two writers submissions, am I going to look at the one who has learned the basic rules and sends me a proper query with all the information I need to make a decision? Or the writer that sends a paragraph saying: here's my manuscript, it's fricken awesome, let me know what you think. Trust me, even if you plan on self-publish, learning how to write an enticing query for your project makes you a better writer, it gives you insights into the project to make the project better. It makes you ask yourself the hard questions. The questions editors and publishers, bloggers and reviewers must ask.

Chapter 5

"WHO ARE YOU WRITING FOR?"

You can either do what you want and write for yourself, or you can do what the market wants and write for others. Neither option is a bogus one. They're both two sides of the same coin.

Doing What You Want:
Means that what you put down on paper is the stuff YOU want to write. Even though you may or may not make money from this, it should be looked at as more of a lifestyle than a business. What you end up writing will most likely be a fiction novel or a memoir about your life, or even some kind of non-fiction topic you're passionate about and well versed in. Your not writing something like your a robot with the intent of producing what pop fiction junkies want, or anything else that is currently raking in money.

The pros to this method are numerous, but a couple hot points are:

1) Putting down on paper what you want is more enjoyable. You're writing the material you'd want to read, or teaching people the science of your wild and crazy life story. It really ain't work, its more like playtime. That's why its a lifestyle.

2) When your doing what you want, you end up writing what your well schooled in, which makes any effort a tasty piece of cake. You ain't gotta get your book nerd on that much because your life experiences are the research. You ain't gotta read a lot of other shit you don't want to, just so you can learn the science of how others did it before you.

Putting ink down on paper for what you want means that as soon as it dries, its gonna be infinitely times better than anything else you could have done. Trust in the schooling we laid down to you in examples 1 and 2 above, and just know that when you scribble down what you want, it will inherently pack a much more powerful oomph.

Doing What The Market Wants

Is you getting the science on what's raking in the big bucks right now, then transforming into a robot and pumping out a book in that genre, not cause you dig it, but cause your betting on the chance to rake in the big bucks. This method is a business model, not a lifestyle. Unless you're lucky enough to enjoy writing what's trending. Think about when Twilight hit the market, and the next thing you know book stores everywhere were flooded with the garbage of angsty emo teenage-vampire love stories.

It is a solid hustle, just as solid as writing the material you'd wanna read. But the truth is, it sucks and its fucking boring as all hell, at least to me. You gotta get your book nerd on hella hardcore. Way to much research will be needed. And its a gamble that may not pay out what your expecting.

You ain't gonna see that kinda shoddy ass work used for successful nonfiction. the time and energy that you will need to put into researching a non-fiction book that covers a topic you don't know anything about is just dumb, no offense. Books that rake in money and draw a large pool of readers in non-fiction categories aren't written by some ignorant cats who don't know anything about the topics going into it. Its successful cause those cats already have the science on the subject matter: they've spent years going to school, usually majoring in the specific field of their topic. Plus they most likely have hands on experience with it in the real world, and not to mention a real love for the subject matter.

George here, I wouldn't call it dumb if you have a fair amount of experience in the field. However, these type of projects do require on average, a year or two of research and another year of editing. At least that's been my experience with the non fiction I've written.

Vinnie here, like I said: dumb!

Writing fiction you don't read or care about is another matter entirely, and can actually be a solid business plan. But that's exactly what it is, a business plan, not a lifestyle. You've got a built in market for it, after all. But check it, without the boom of something like Twilight or 50 Shades of Gray to inform you of what's popular, the hassle of really finding what genre is raking in the dough at that moment in time can be extremely difficult in our circumstance. Although Geo just said Cadmus will be spitting this out in future newsletters. Then you gotta buy a bunch of it. Next you gotta read these books you just dumped money into, but as a textbook instead of for pleasure, just so you can get a grip on the style. Then you gotta do some more of that dreaded internet research. Finally you gotta try your hand at writing something that will be worth a shit to sell, cause to be frank you simply might not have the skills to sit down with out any passion for the project, and mechanically pump out something of value in that particular style. Geo and I ain't gonna be writing any 50 Shades Of Gray or Twilight type of shit anytime soon, ya dig? But you may see some hard ass convict fiction, Eddie Bunker style. Long story short, write what you know.

 Anyways, this gives you some experienced insights to consider. Just be prepared for the process to become a real bitch cause you most likely won't have a way to access the resources your gonna need, but hey, maybe Cadmus will add writers research to their services? if you got it like that (you sly convict you), here's some spots you can roll through to see what genres are raking in the big bucks:
 - Amazon.com (just look at sales numbers for the different genres)
 - AuthorEarnings.com
 - TheCreativePenn.com/genre
 Geo here,
 When I landed on the row and looked around for a hustle I knew I was in deep shit. I couldn't draw and wasn't going to do laundry, not that there's anything wrong with that. For me, once I decided to roll the dice and my dollars I focused on writing for money, identifying resources for people in prisons. Back in 2008 they were damn hard to find. At least up to date, reliable resources. And I starved the first three years, nearly gave up every week but I couldn't. I had no choice. Aren't you glad. Lol.....

Chapter 6

"PULLING YOUR OWN WEIGHT"

 You gotta make sure that what your putting out to the world has value. It needs to be well written, steady paced, have good characterization, and a whole slew of other stuff. This is a PROFESSION, and it needs to be treated as such. We would suggest that in your free time, instead of watching TV, playing cards, or hanging out, you read. Read lots and lots of books. Its enjoyable, but your also working at your profession, because your gaining the science on how others do it. Your also removing yourself from any potential yard drama you might get wrapped up in. Once you start putting yourself out there as a public figure in the publishing world, you need to be taken seriously. Getting written up for failing U.A's, or constantly fighting (like Vinnie) presents an unreliable persona. And at least here in Arizona, they post all your tickets on their website so any agents or journalist have access to your business. Besides there's a time to put away childish things, and this is the time. So become a hermit in your cell, and read more while doing it.

 Reading more means that you'll also begin to develop an almost sixth sense of what makes a book enjoyable or not. Take the Odd Thomas series by Dean Koontz. The first couple books were awesome, and really enjoyable. But somewhere in there, Dean or whatever ghostwriter he was using really screwed up our paranormal investigating friend Odds story. It became tacky and rushed. It almost had a feel like a child had written it.

 We would also suggest reading more books on how to actually WRITE. If you have author workshop programs at your prison

SELL YOUR BOOKS FROM PRISON

unit, sign up for em. If you can find any good author correspondence courses, sign up for em. Even if they cost a bit of money, its worth it. Every little bit that you can do to improve your craft, do it.

Finally, if you choose to publish through Cadmus, listen to what were telling you. Don't fight us on every little thing because you think your right. If we say something you disagree with, just know that we're saying it for a reason. It isn't because we're egotistical and think we know everything, its because at this point in time of your career we know better than you do in these circumstances. We aren't trying to sabotage your book, or your career. This is a business, and we don't succeed unless you succeed. So its in our best interest that you make as much money as possible. So please, when we tell you something, accept it. We've been doing this for A LONG FUCKIN TIME, we know our stuff. After we've been working together for a while, you too will know your stuff, and will have a Ph.D. in this publishing game. That will make for an excellent author/publisher relationship between us while working on your future books. Things will be done faster, and everyone involved will profit more in the end. But for this first one or two books you publish with us, let us drive the car while you watch and learn.

Chapter 7

WRITE A BOOK IN 30 DAYS? YO, STEP OFF!

Bull shit, I used to think. But your holding a 34 day book. George here, if you have even a passing interest in writing, these '30 day book' stories have caught your attention as mine. I was never a prolific writer, being dyslexic, writing has always been difficult for me and rarely enjoyable, thank God for tablets. If I had to describe me as a writer I'd say I'm a working writer with a splash of inspirational writer. In other words, if I wanted to buy store and shoes I had to write to pay for them. My favorite writing is inspirational, like this missive. It wasn't a planned part of this book. Yesterday Vinnie and I were talking about having seven days to finish this book. He said 'we got this player' we can send it to Ken Thursday Nov 30th. I said you misunderstood, the book is suppose to be in print Dec 1st. We still have to finish the last 8 chapters, do Resources, Glossary, About the Authors, FAQs, Blurbs, finish the custom cover, ISBN #, LCCN, layout, approve the proof and upload it. One of us said something about, we should put that in the book, about how this project was done in 30 days. So here I am, 3:30 am writing about it, Lol.

Update:
To further complicate our progress, we are in the middle of our Black Friday sale, I have a full-time job and Vinnie has bipolar issues. Once during our writing journey Vinnie slept for two days. I never said a word about it, he woke up, got showered and caffeinated and went back to writing. There were days Vinnie wanted me to review and edit content and Cadmus clients had to come first. I mention this to illustrate life is guaranteed to drop

SELL YOUR BOOKS FROM PRISON

stinky circumstances in your path like that person who keeps doing a 'drive by' in front of my house. If I ever catch em I'm duct taping their ass to the toilet.

    Rumor is, it's Vinnie. The many benefits of this challenge is you learn.... a lot about not only writing but yourself. Are you going to quit a few days into it, two weeks, the third week? Few will ever finish this challenge in 30 days and that's the point. You learn that quality writing, for most of can't be rushed. You learn how well you know your subject material, in my case, writing and marketing is what I've done for 14 years so I know this stuff off the top of my head. Experience is paramount when writing a book in 30 days unless your writing about being a dumb ass and learning how to do something, think of those ' Idiots Guide to Knitting' Or How to Catch a Stinky Drive By. Hey, if you write that book I'll buy a copy.

    Update:
Like many a writer, we got sidetracked with life and those pesky edits. It is now already April 2024. Damn.

Chapter 8

THE SECRET SAUCE: EDITING

You finished your book. THAT'S FANTASTIC! You wrote it all down, made sure you went real slow in order to reduce a boat load of spelling and grammatical errors. THAT'S AWESOME! You sped read though it to make sure you didn't forget a line or two. THAT'S AMAZING! All that's left is to throw it in a manila envelope with Cadmus's address on it, slap a stamp on that sucker, and drop it in the mail on your way to chow. THATS ALL INCREDIBLY WRONG!

You got the first part correct, but you lost it after that. After you write that bad boy, you gotta set it aside for a little bit. After a period of time, three days to two weeks, pick that bitch back up, and SLOWLY read it. Unfortunately, or Fortunately your gonna notice that your drop dead sexy manuscript might in fact be.... a barfly. You see, during the creation and construction of your story, you will suffer from what we call in the biz, "beer goggles". That fresh first draft of your manuscript is going to be the most beautiful thing you've ever seen in your life. It will have no flaws, no warts, and no blemishes... all because you'll be so drunk on the happiness of completing your manuscript.

After you've set your book aside for a few weeks to a month, you need to doff your plastic surgeons cap, and take that baby in for a face lift! You will notice that once you read it, you'll see how you can make it better. You'll see what needs to be striked out, if any scenes need to be added, if you need to reword certain sentence structures, hell maybe lose an unnecessary chapter, or maybe even add one. Only you can do this though. Not your homeboys or homegirls on the cell block with you, and not Cadmus when you mail it to us.

For me, I enjoy revising my work. I enjoy it more than the concept creation, and first draft. I know that when I pick my manuscript up after a time, is when the real fun starts. Unfortunately, I've learned the hard way that you need to set a revision limit for yourself. We would suggest no more than 3 revisions. You can get into a revision rut, to where every time you look at your manuscript you find something that you believe could be better, or think of new chapters to add. Next thing you know, its 2 years later and your basically still writing your manuscript. There is a such thing as too much plastic surgery. Just look at Lil Kim and Mickey Rourke... holy shit.

George here, this is one of the secrets between a crap or okay book and book that sparkles, that induces the reader to turn that page. How many boring ass books have you read on writing or selling your book?
We've read them too. We wanted to make this book different, like
IntraFuckingresting. And it is interesting because as a reader you don't have a clue what kind of crazy antidotes one of us will drop next.
And you can't guess how many times we have reviewed, edited these pages. Venue and I have checked these pages at least three to five times each. That's the secret magic, time. Give your brain time away from from your creation, every parent needs time away from the kid in order to appreciate it.
 A Guide to Copy Editing, Content/Graphics Editing, and Continuity/Story Flow

Writing a book is a labor of love, but the true magic often happens during the editing process. The careful scrutiny and refinement of a manuscript ensure that the author's vision is communicated effectively. Among the various editing stages, three crucial types stand out: copy editing, content/graphics editing, and continuity/story flow editing.

Copy Editing:

Copy editing is the meticulous process of reviewing a manuscript for errors and inconsistencies in grammar, punctuation, spelling, and style. This type of editing is the last line of defense before a manuscript goes to print or is published digitally. Copy editors dive into the nitty-gritty details of language, aiming to enhance clarity, coherence, and correctness.

During copy editing, editors scrutinize sentence structures, correct grammatical errors, and ensure that the text adheres to a consistent style guide. This stage is also an opportunity to address typographical issues, such as font inconsistencies and formatting glitches. The goal is not just to catch errors but to polish the prose, creating a seamless reading experience for the audience.

Content/Graphics Editing:

Content and graphics editing goes beyond the realm of words, focusing on the overall visual and conceptual elements of a book. This type of editing is particularly crucial for works that incorporate images, graphs, charts, or any visual content. Editors in this domain work to ensure that visual elements align with the text, enhancing comprehension and engagement.

In content/graphics editing, the editor assesses the visual appeal, relevance, and placement of images within the text. They also verify that captions accurately describe the visuals and that graphics complement the narrative rather than detract from it. This process aims to create a harmonious blend of text and visuals, enhancing the overall impact of the book.

Continuity/Story Flow Editing:

While copy editing polishes the language, and content/graphics editing enhances visual elements, continuity/story flow editing focuses on the broader narrative structure. This type of editing addresses the coherence of the story, ensuring that plotlines, characters, and themes align seamlessly throughout the book.

Editors engaged in continuity/story flow editing assess the pacing of the narrative, identify plot holes, and evaluate character development. They also pay attention to the overall structure, assessing the logical progression of chapters and scenes. This editing stage aims to create a compelling and immersive reading experience by addressing any disruptions or inconsistencies in the storyline.

Each of these editing types plays a unique and indispensable role in refining a manuscript. Authors and editors collaborate to ensure that the final product is a polished, cohesive, and engaging piece of work. While copy editing fine-tunes the language, content/graphics editing enhances the visual appeal, and continuity/story flow editing weaves everything together into a seamless narrative.

In the dynamic world of book editing, these three stages work in tandem to elevate a manuscript to its full potential. Authors, armed with a deeper understanding of each type of editing, can collaborate more effectively with their editorial team. The result is a book that not only meets the highest standards of quality but also captivates and resonates with its intended audience.

Chapter 9

THE POWER OF THE QUERY LETTER

Even if you plan on self-publishing, <u>don't skip this lesson</u>

In the competitive world of book publishing, the first step to getting your manuscript noticed is often through a well-crafted query letter. This brief document serves as your book's ambassador, representing your writing skills and the essence of your story to potential publishers. Here's a guide on how to write an effective query letter that captures the attention of publishers and increases your chances of getting your book into print.

Research Your Target Publishers:
Before you start writing your query letter, research publishers who specialize in your genre. Tailoring your query to the preferences of specific publishers demonstrates that you've done your homework and increases the likelihood of finding the right match for your manuscript.

Create a Strong Opening:
Begin your query with a compelling hook that immediately grabs the publisher's attention. Whether it's an intriguing question, a surprising fact, or a brief summary of your book's unique selling point, make sure it's engaging and relevant to your story.

Introduce Yourself
Provide a brief introduction of yourself, emphasizing any relevant writing credentials, publishing credits, or experiences that make you uniquely qualified to write this book. Be concise and focus on what makes you the ideal author for your particular work.

SELL YOUR BOOKS FROM PRISON

Synopsis of Your Book:
Clearly and succinctly summarize your book in a paragraph or two. Highlight the main characters, the central conflict, and the unique elements that set your story apart. Avoid spoilers and focus on creating a sense of intrigue that leaves the publisher wanting to know more.

Highlight the Marketability:
Publishers want to know that your book has commercial potential. Discuss your target audience, market trends, and any comparable titles that have been successful. This demonstrates that you understand the market and have a strategic plan for positioning your book.

Showcase Your Platform:
Publishers are often interested in an author's platform, which includes your online presence, social media following, and any other avenues through which you can promote your book. Briefly mention your platform and how you plan to contribute to the marketing efforts.

Include a Call to Action:
Conclude your query letter with a clear call to action. Invite the publisher to request the full manuscript, and express your enthusiasm about the possibility of working with them. Make sure to thank them for their time and consideration.

Polish and Proofread:
Your query letter is a reflection of your writing skills, so ensure it is polished and free of errors. Proofread carefully for grammar, spelling, and formatting. A well-presented query letter indicates professionalism and attention to detail.

Follow Submission Guidelines:
Different publishers may have specific submission guidelines, so be sure to follow them meticulously. This includes formatting, preferred submission method, and any additional materials they may request.

Personalize Each Query:
Avoid sending out generic query letters to multiple publishers. Personalize each query to the specific publisher, referencing why you believe your book is a good fit for their list. This extra effort shows that you are genuinely interested in their publishing house.

In the competitive world of book publishing, a well-crafted query letter can make the difference between your manuscript being overlooked or landing on a publisher's desk for further consideration. By following these guidelines, you can increase your chances of making a positive impression and taking the first step toward seeing your book in print.

Chapter 10

"TAKING YOUR MS FOR A JOY RIDE"

Once you've reached your limit of revisions on your manuscript, you gotta take that baby out for a joy ride! This means finding "beta readers", cats you recruit to read your manuscript with the purpose of giving you their 2 cents on the product. Their like the fiends a dealer brings in to test a new batch after a re-up so they can give a 1 to 10 rating on the product.

In the case of beta readers, most folks first choice will be to slide it over to their homies, and that's fine if said cats are capable of being brutally honest with their friends. But unfortunately/fortunately our friends don't usually wanna hurt our feelings, so they will lie to us in order to preserve the relationship. There is also the factor of favoritism between friends. Most of the time friendship can cloud folks perspective, and they will be unable to see a negative in their homies, their actions, or anything they may produce.

The best people to recruit as beta readers are cats you don't even know. If you have an actual library at your unit, while your in their try and clock the regular faces. If you don't have a unit Library, try and identify people on your cell block that do a lot of reading. Once you've accomplished either of those you can then, respectfully, approach them and introduce yourself. Inform them that your an author, and you need impartial beta readers to take your manuscript for a joy ride. Ask them if they wouldn't mind reading it, and giving you their input. Its probably best to devise a "survey" of questions to give them that they can answer about your book, as well as a blank section for their general opinions.

GEORGE R. KAYER AND VINNIE VALE

The questions should be short and specific, as well as easy to answer. You don't wanna drowned them in your neediness. This is also a form of publicity, because if they really enjoy your manuscript, the may became a fan of your pervious or future books. Once you get these cats feedback, put it to good use. Fix what needs to be fixed. They may in fact spot things you overlooked during your revisions. You also have to remember that, its YOUR book, not theirs. Just cause they suggest something be changed or added, doesn't mean their correct. Although, if I had 5 beta readers, and all 5 of them made the same suggestion on something I disagreed with, I would make the revision no matter how much I loved the original.

George here,
Staring at the wall, that's what the guards thought I was doing. Before tablets I had to write everything by hand, the paper was white and the walls were nearly as white. Back when I published Inmate Shopper from my cell, (20 years in solitary) there would come a point with each new edition where I had to spread out the pages to grasp a proper layout. I'd have 160 pages in a pile but just couldn't get the full experience of how that issue should flow. I'd mop the floor, clear off the bunk and begin laying out the pages, even tapping 20 or 30 to the wall. I normally did this after lights out, the paper blended into the wall under the subdued light so when guards did their walk it looked to them like I was just staring at the wall. Even had a few ask: are you okay? Most didn't care as long as I was breathing, upright or not.

But for me, to beta read the project I had to spread it out, only then could I see what pages or content were out of place and needed to be moved. The point is, do what you gotta do to get it right.

Online beta readers.
This is one of the features we want to add to the new Interactive Bookstore at Books By Prisoners. Probably, will do something like a chapter at a time..

I'm not a fan of posting ones whole manuscript for the world to steal before it is published.

And of course, if you would like Cadmus to post a chapter of

SELL YOUR BOOKS FROM PRISON

your manuscript on a beta readers site or two, these services are available.

Alrighty then, stop staring at the damn wall and get back to work!!

Chapter 11

"GETTING YOUR BOOK COVER SLUNG DOWN"

Never believe that bullshit "don't judge a book by its cover". They taught us all that in elementary school so we wouldn't exclude others cause we judged them as different. Which obviously worked real well, because our country is so united.... I mean, if you were to ever meet Vinnie in person, I bet you'd never believe in a million years that he's a former 3 time national, 1 time world "Edging" champion. But guess what, you'd be absolutely correct.

Anyways, the cover is the first damn thing you see when you look at a book! Of course you judge a book by the cover. Appearance is everything in the marketing game. If you wrote a prison cook book titled "69 Prison Ramen Recipes", and then decided to use the poop emoji as your cover image, no one will buy that literal shit. A good eye catching cover is one of the most important aspects of book marketing. And why book cover designers can get up to $5,000.

Book covers fundamentally exist solely for the purpose of marketing and selling books. If they weren't so necessary, every Stephen King book would be solid white, with his name on the bottom and the title right above it saying "Book #1/2/3/etc.", in the numerical order he published them. Publishers like Random House, Nolo and Cadmus wouldn't have a pocket full of book designers on staff. At Cadmus, no less than four people assist with the design of each book cover.

How many times have you yourself glanced over a book because the cover didn't attract you? Then, later in life ended up

SELL YOUR BOOKS FROM PRISON

reading said book only to find out it was excellent?

    You want your books' cover to not only represent the spirit of its contents, you also want it to turn as many heads as possible with out being to gaudy. You want your books cover to be as eye catching as Kim Kardashian in a thong bikini, or Dwayne "The Rock" Johnson in a speedo (sorry for that visual fellas, but heterosexual lady convicts write books to). You want that cover to be like John Gotti struttin out of a court house after being acquitted for the umpteenth time at trial, all decked out in a $10,000 dollar Gucci suit, just dripping in swagger and style. You want your book to ooze confidence like the Dapper Don himself. When peeps look at your book cover, you want it to whisper at them seductively "you know you wanna come and crack my spine open".

Do publishers let authors decide what's on the cover?

    When referring to Traditional Publishers, no. They are spending their money to publish your manuscript. They have experts in every department that live book covers every day. If you are using a publishing service that provides a cover service, you most likely may have a say in your book cover. Some companies will put anything you want on a cover, others may not. If your cover is a sensitive part of your book have a cover discussion before you sign a contract.
    At Cadmus, we take author suggestions into account and have the designers work with their theme. Of course on AI and custom designed covers authors have more input but if we feel the authors ideas are not consistent with market trends we may have a discussion about that.

    On the following pages are an example of an ai and composite book covers. These are the ultimate covers in design and technology, cost runs $300 to $500.

GEORGE R. KAYER AND VINNIE VALE

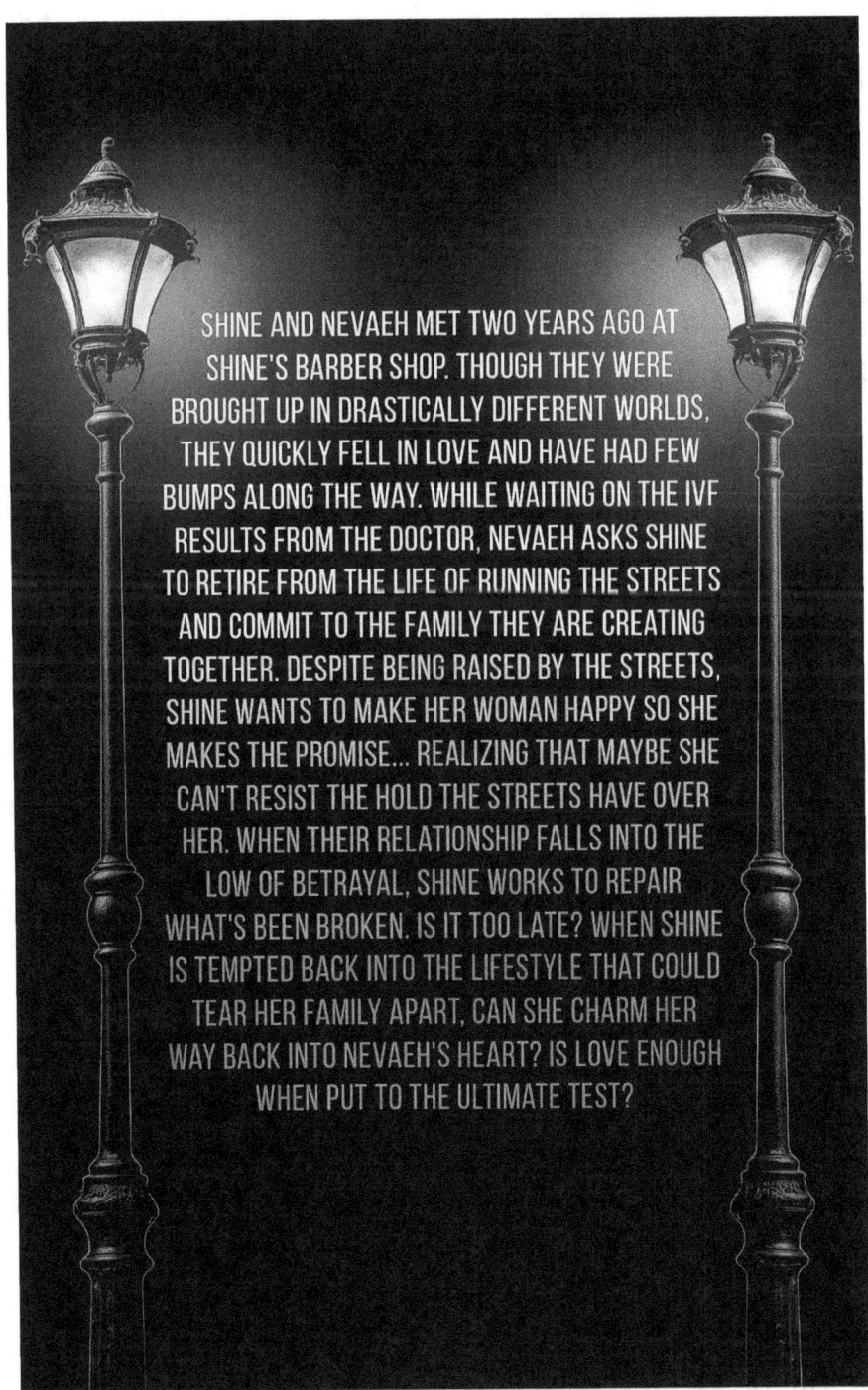

SHINE AND NEVAEH MET TWO YEARS AGO AT SHINE'S BARBER SHOP. THOUGH THEY WERE BROUGHT UP IN DRASTICALLY DIFFERENT WORLDS, THEY QUICKLY FELL IN LOVE AND HAVE HAD FEW BUMPS ALONG THE WAY. WHILE WAITING ON THE IVF RESULTS FROM THE DOCTOR, NEVAEH ASKS SHINE TO RETIRE FROM THE LIFE OF RUNNING THE STREETS AND COMMIT TO THE FAMILY THEY ARE CREATING TOGETHER. DESPITE BEING RAISED BY THE STREETS, SHINE WANTS TO MAKE HER WOMAN HAPPY SO SHE MAKES THE PROMISE... REALIZING THAT MAYBE SHE CAN'T RESIST THE HOLD THE STREETS HAVE OVER HER. WHEN THEIR RELATIONSHIP FALLS INTO THE LOW OF BETRAYAL, SHINE WORKS TO REPAIR WHAT'S BEEN BROKEN. IS IT TOO LATE? WHEN SHINE IS TEMPTED BACK INTO THE LIFESTYLE THAT COULD TEAR HER FAMILY APART, CAN SHE CHARM HER WAY BACK INTO NEVAEH'S HEART? IS LOVE ENOUGH WHEN PUT TO THE ULTIMATE TEST?

Richard L. Tabler is an individual that made serious mistakes in and throughout his life before finding the strength to write his own first book, "Within the Shadows of Life", in 2021. Those mistakes have cost him his freedom, and pain and suffering for others. It wasn't until Mr. Tabler turned 43-years-old that he was able to forgive himself and love himself to fully accept Jesus Christ into his life and heart. It's through the Grace of God that he is able to write the book you now hold in your hand and that those in society live and care about Mr. Tabler's voice as he suffers from survivors' guilt here on Texas' Death Row.

SELL YOUR BOOKS FROM PRISON

Chapter 12

TITLE? OH MY TITLE, WHERE ART THOU ?

Vinnie here, let's talk a little bit about names and titles. This is gonna be fun, cause its gonna allow me to use all kinds of references to yard nicknames and stuff. Like what makes a good nickname? Amongst his friends, George is known as "Geo". Pretty cool right? Real simple and straight to the point. You need nothing more in a nickname. Myself on the other hand spent over a decade involved with a white prison "union" if you catch my drift, and by way of my actions, I earned the nickname "Chaos". Also real simple and straight to the point, but not a very good one. That's not the kinda name you want if you wish to attract lasting friendships outside of that lifestyle. It sounds cool and scary, but it doesn't really pull "none active" folks into my circle of trust, cause their mostly gonna be on edge while waiting to see why I earned that nickname.

Books are the same way. You need a good title, one that sums up the spirit of your book in as few words as possible. Something that's an attention grabber, but isn't offensive or putt-off'ish, ya dig? Its like when we illustrated using the poo emoji as the cover for your hypothetical prison cook book. Nobody wants to equate poo with ramen noodle soup. Well... sadly there are some sick puppies that would probably enjoy something like that, but that's a situation for a psychiatrist to dissect, not us.

Think of a classic title for something that pulled you in cause it sounded cool, and at the same time summed up the spirit of the material it represented. How about the classic Hip Hop album "Life After Death" by the Notorious B.I.G? It came out right after his murder, it summed up the body of his work up until that point as well as after, and it struck a cord because of the unfortunate event that led up to its release. How about the movie "Men Who Stare At Goats"? What an infesting title, it not only summed up the movie, it was an attention grabber. People saw it and said "what the hell is this?!?" That's what you want your book title to be. Iconic, memorable, original.

Thanks Vinnie, that was a memorable puff piece intro, or should I say poop piece intro? Now let's get to work. The number one mistake made by self published authors is the title. It is not their fault, generally. It took me 14 years to learn all the tricks, tactics and secrets I share in this book and it would he egotistical for me to condemn folks for a lack of knowledge.

And giving credit where it's due, as I become more familiar with our 600 authors, I've found some excellent, spot on titles.

If you have any money in your budget for professional title research, Do it. I have listed the first five tricks-tactics-secrets as the basics, these basics can be used whether or not you have funds for a professional title research.

Here's my 5 Tricks, Tactics and Secrets for choosing the correct title.

These apply to all genres, all title considerations. Later in this chapter I impart Tips tactics and secrets for nonfiction.

1. Know that choosing a title is the most important decision for the success of your book.

2. This is Business ! Leave your personal feelings out in the barn with the rest of the manure.

3. Be honest, with yourself. How well do you know the genre (subject matter) of books in your genre? Do you eat, breath and sleep the genre of your book? As an example: Adult Fiction, did you know there are 100+ categories of adult fiction? You say my book is Romance category. And I say, did you know there are 12+ categories of Adult Fiction Romance? Have you read at least four of these categories, did you make a list of the titles you liked, the covers, each synopsis, romantic song titles, movie titles? Or did

you just wake up one day and say to self, today we are going to write a suspenseful romantic fiction with a paranormal twist and thought ghost divorce is an excellent title?

My point is, if you don't know what genre means, or how to correctly identify your books sub genre's your not qualified to choose a title.

4. Trending, what is hot, what are people looking to read for the last three months, the next six months? Choosing a trending title has risk, like not trending in three months. Just like at the casino, players can come across a hot slot or craps table but what's hot today will eventually cool off. There's arguments for both choices of titles: traditional and trending.

5. What do keywords have to do with my title? Everything!!!!!- Just because your book is on Amazon does not mean anyone will see it. When people search for books they type into the search bar these trending words I spoke of earlier because that's what consumers are programmed to do. If your title doesn't have one or four of those keywords it may never pop up in Amazon's search results. That means: No Sales :(

Bonus Tip:
Did you know that book titles, song titles and names of movies are not copyrightable? This means you can use all or part of these, as long as it isn't Trademarked. Trending titles of songs, books and movies in your genre provide you with millions of dollars of free research. Publishers of music, movies and books spend big stacks on titles and for good reason, they know a good title can be all the difference between success and failure. These titles are the first step to identifying the best keywords to reach potential buyers in your genre. Chapter 10 part 2. Title.

NONFICTION TITLES:
Do Not Over think this. If your nonfiction title is over 8 words it's probably wrong. Here are some examples of perfect titles:
Mama's Baby Egg
Sell Your Books From Prison, Rescued From Myself
Write And Get Paid, This Shit Crazy
Start A Non Profit, 100 Ways To Make Money in Prison

SELL YOUR BOOKS FROM PRISON

Legal Guide For Writers, Defund DOC
College For Convicts. Sexually Violent Predator
Complete Guide To Getting Grants. Broken Grace
Snail Mail Penpaling. Luckily Fish Don't Need Raincoats
50 Careers Without A Four Year Degree

 Everyone of these titles is from a published book or magazine: authors in prison. The title tells us exactly what the publication is about in five words or less.
 If you over think a non fiction title it will fall on death ears, it will miss the bullseye.. This is not the time to get clever or cryptic. If you must, place it in the subtitle although, the subtitle should be used for the keywords to optimize customer searches for sales.

 Choosing the right title for a book is a crucial step in the publishing process. A well-crafted title not only captures the essence of the content but also plays a significant role in attracting potential readers. Keyword research, commonly associated with SEO (Search Engine Optimization), can be a valuable tool in the process of selecting a book title. Here are five reasons or benefits of using keyword research for this purpose:

Enhances Discoverability and Visibility:
 One of the primary advantages of using keyword research for choosing a book title is the improvement in discoverabilty. Keywords are the terms and phrases that potential readers use when searching for books online. By incorporating relevant keywords into your title, you increase the likelihood of your book appearing in search results.

 For example, if your book is a mystery novel set in a small town, including keywords like "small town mystery" or "mysterious town" in your title can make it more visible to readers interested in that genre. This not only helps your book stand out among similar titles but also ensures that it reaches the right audience.

Connects with Target Audience:

Keyword research provides insights into the language and preferences of your target audience. By understanding the terms they commonly use or are likely to search for, you can tailor your book title to resonate with them. This connection is vital for grabbing the attention of potential readers and making them curious about your book.

For instance, if your book is a self-help guide for young professionals, keywords like "career success," "personal development," or "millennial empowerment" could be integrated into the title. This not only makes your book more appealing to your target audience but also communicates the value it offers to them.

Optimizes for Online Platforms:

In the digital age, a significant portion of book discovery and sales happens online. Whether it's on e-commerce platforms, search engines, or social media, having a title optimized with relevant keywords ensures that your book is well-positioned for success in these spaces. Potential readers often use search engines to find books, and a keyword-optimized title increases the chances of your book appearing in their search results.

Additionally, social media platforms use algorithms that consider keywords when displaying content to users. A title with strategically chosen keywords can increase the visibility of your book on these platforms, leading to more engagement and potential sales.

Competitive Edge in the Market:

The book market can be highly competitive, with numerous titles vying for readers' attention. Keyword research allows you to analyze the titles of similar books and identify gaps or opportunities. By choosing a title that not only reflects the content of your book but also incorporates keywords that are less saturated or more niche, you can gain a competitive edge.

For example, if you find that many books in your genre use similar keywords in their titles, you might explore alternative terms or combinations that still accurately represent your book but have less competition. This uniqueness can make your book stand out in a crowded marketplace.

Facilitates Marketing and Promotion:
Effective marketing is essential for the success of any book, and a well-chosen title can significantly aid in promotional efforts. Keywords that are commonly searched for or trending can be integrated into your book title to align with current interests and capitalize on existing market trends.

Moreover, a keyword-optimized title provides a foundation for creating compelling marketing materials. From online ads to social media posts, having a title that incorporates relevant keywords allows you to create content that resonates with potential readers and encourages them to explore your book further.

In conclusion, utilizing keyword research to choose a book title offers a range of benefits that contribute to the overall success of a book. From improving discoverability and connecting with the target audience to optimizing for online platforms, gaining a competitive edge, and facilitating effective marketing, the strategic use of keywords enhances the visibility and appeal of your book in a competitive literary landscape.

Shit Titles:
Using four letter words, as in foul language in your title is always an option, as long as you understand why? Ask yourself why am I considering using a curse word in my title? There are three legit reasons to do so.
1. To express anger.
2. To express humor.
3. A marketing ploy to gain attention.

Below are the top selling books with the word Shit in their titles.
1. How to Stop Losing Your Shit With Your Kids: A Practical Guide to Becoming a Calmer, Happier Parent.

2. Shit Actually: The Definitive, 100% Objective Guide To Modern Cinema.

3. Tough Shit: Life Advice From a Fat Lazy Slob Who Did Good.

4. Do Epic Shit.

5. Get Your Shit Together.

I think the first two were professionally title researched. The third is just one of those natural titles that work well. The fourth and fifth titles could be self published because they don't take advantage of a powerful sub title. They're missing out on grabbing the attention of not just readers but the search engines too.

Chapter 13

THE LAYOUTS

We've covered a lot of yards on the gridiron of publishing. So far - editing, beta readers, covers, titles - all important aspects of marketing and we're almost to the end zone. We gotta cover a few more things, that way we don't get sacked in a blitz by our ignorance. Yes, as I write this, it is football season.

What is Layout?
Okay, grab a book, open to the beginning of any chapter. Notice the header, ie., the chapter title, notice how the font is a different size and perhaps a different style than the body of text? Now notice the margins, those blank spaces all around the text, and then the bottom footer, that's where the page number and footnotes are printed.

Looks simple doesn't it. Heck ya, my family member could do my layout. Just like Tom Brady made making touchdowns look easy or Martha Stewart makes cooking look easy, it is not. There's a lot of the layout puzzle I didn't mention because this isn't a book about page layouts and, the layout process is included in all Cadmus Publishing packages.

The book layout is marketing, it is how the words the authors write are framed. How many words are on a page, page size, headers and it should make the reader feel comfortable. We only notice a layout when it is done incorrectly.

On the flip side, we are not saying just anyone can provide

a proper layout of ones book. Like every step in the publishing process, Experience matters.

    We can't stress enough that the folks you have turn your MS into pages for your readers, be professionals. It needs to look GOOD, and recruited neophytes will most likely be unable to do even a passable slapstick job at it. It's possible, but your gonna have to rely on your trust in the individual you've recruited to do it for you. It needs to have flow, your mind and eyes shouldn't have to be forced into focusing on each sentence. We've all opened a book with tiny print all crammed together.

    Let's try an exercise shall we. Grab a book off your shelf, any book you have in the genre you'll be publishing in. Open it up and scope it out, what's it look like? Does it look like dog shit? We doubt it. That baby's got a nice readable font huh? Its all uniformed and undistracting right? We bet your eyes just float down the page smoothly, and you wanna go onto the next page because the words have caught your attention. Well stop that and pull your eyes back to this book, cause we're not yet done here.

    Its the little issues like a crappy layout that can kill a book, and those simple examples above are just the tip of the iceberg when it comes to layout. Don't become a proverbial Titanic and get sunk by the rest of that big bitch hidden under the waves. When peeps pick your book up and scan through it, or use the "Peek Inside" option online, don't let their eyes be assaulted with layout chaos. Anarchy is cool in all, but not when it comes to writing and publishing books. You want yours to be a piece of art, front to back.

    We're still on the first impressions stage here, and if folks aren't stimulated by the visual, they ain't gonna wanna get to know the "real you", ya dig? Ask Vinnie... he's a big, slung down, fat scary white guy so he has to rely on being funny and charismatic to attract people. Books can't really do that, so their all about the aesthetic at first. You want your book to be a Playboy Centerfold, or the Peoples Sexiest Man Alive.

THE SHOT CALLER—Part Three

Chapter 14

ALL ABOUT THE BENJAMIN'S BABY? MAYBE NOT.......

We're almost there y'all! Damn its taking along time, and you've probably already skipped over all this technical pre-publishing shit straight to the juicy marketing stuff. For those of you who've stuck with Geo and I, you've earned our Love and Respect. And, you're already leaps and bounds ahead of the other cats who just skipped the first half.

This chapter is the good stuff, the thing everyone wants to talk about...THE DEAD PRESIDENTS! Specifically, how many of them old dead white dudes should you charge for your book?

One hustle is to shoot that price through the roof, creating a thing called "Percieved Value". That's the hustle used by company's such as Gucci, or Rolls Royce. Its the business scheme that folks will see a jacked up price and assume its of greater substance or material. In things like books, it implies its of a higher quality, has more popularity, is a better story than its counterparts, or even a better return policy. Common human nature is to think that something priced higher than items equal in all other aspects, is for some reason "better". Its done throughout all industries, and even in things like politics. A high price usually means less than average sales, but it also means higher royalties!

Another hustle is to set that price low as hell, that way you can try and entice more cats into buying your book. That means you push more product, therefore making more royalties. That also means more cats that could potentially recommend it to others, ergo, more sales and profit.

Finally, the third hustle is a combo of the other 2. You start off by pricing your book low to draw folks in, and build up word of mouth. Then, once it gains its stride in sales, you begin to raise the price ever so gently until you arrive at the desired goal.

Your gonna run into roadblocks with how cheap you can set the price of your books. You always wanna make sure that however low you set it you still pull in some royalties, that way you can at least break even or cover the cost of the ad campaign. Don't forget, there's gonna be cats gettin into your pocket on each sale. There's printing costs, the retailers percentage, etc. A lot that goes into it. I'm gonna let Geo take over here for a minute.

Can I set my own price?
I have a two part answer for you. First, if you publish with Cadmus, pricing your book is part of our services. We will have a pricing discussion to consider the best pricing, marketing strategy for your budget and book.

Second, authors who self publish are the boss. Ultimately you decide nearly every detail about your book, including pricing. We provide what you need to know here to make competent pricing decisions but would caution you to also listen if we offer specific advice about a pricing strategy for your title, we do this everyday and are aware of marketing trends most people in prisons don't have access to.

Each genre of book contains its own pricing idiosyncrasies Price a legal, medical or business book to low and our human nature tells our subconscious that the book must not be very good.

Every genre has there own price structure with the best known authors commanding the top prices. If your in the non fiction family my best advice is be more concerned about gaining an audience than gaining dollars. A writer or actor without an audience lives a tortured life.

Chapter 15

WHY DOESN'T MY BOOK SELL? "METADATA"

Vinnie here. You're probably like me, and asking yourself the simple question... "what the hell is Metadata?" I had not the slightest clue until beginning this chapter. That's why I did a deep dive into what exactly Metadata is. I learned a lot, and let me tell you something... I am not the cat to school you up on this subject, and just how important it is. Geo is the cat that's gonna need to take you to school on this.. So I'm gonna regurgitate the basic overview in simplistic terms in order to prepare you for the deep dive into the abyss of Metadata.

Basically, Metadata is the info ABOUT your book that search engines look for.. Things such as what genre/subgenre it falls under, what keywords are connected to it, its synopsis your author bio, and its 'BISAC' (Book Industry Standards And Communications) Codes, and so much much more.

This is the point where I should let Geo take the wheel. Congratulations, you are about to be initiated into the science of Metadata magic, why your book sells or doesn't sell.

In the vast sea of books available to readers, metadata serves as the beacon that guides potential readers to discover your work. It acts as the digital DNA of a book, providing essential information that helps it stand out amidst the noise of the publishing world. In the realm of self-publishing, understanding and effectively utilizing metadata can make the difference between obscurity and success.

GEORGE R. KAYER AND VINNIE VALE

At the heart of metadata lies BISAC (Book Industry Standards and Communications) codes, a system developed by the Book Industry Study Group (BISG) that categorizes books based on subject matter. These codes serve as the foundation upon which the rest of the metadata is built. Choosing the most relevant BISAC codes ensures that your book is placed in the appropriate categories, increasing its visibility to potential readers browsing through online retailers and libraries.

Keywords play a crucial role in metadata optimization. These are the terms and phrases that readers are likely to use when searching for books similar to yours. By strategically incorporating relevant keywords into your metadata, you increase the likelihood of your book appearing in search results, thus attracting more potential readers.

An author bio provides readers with insight into the person behind the words. It establishes credibility and fosters a connection between the author and the reader. Including an engaging and informative author bio in your metadata can pique the interest of readers who may be unfamiliar with your work, prompting them to explore further.

The synopsis serves as a teaser, offering a glimpse into the storyline and themes of your book. It should be concise yet compelling, enticing readers to delve deeper into the pages of your work. A well-crafted synopsis can spark curiosity and encourage readers to make a purchase.

Meta tags are like signposts that guide search engines to understand the content of your book. By including relevant meta tags in your metadata, you make it easier for search engines to index and rank your book, increasing its visibility in search results.

When these elements – BISAC codes, keywords, author bio, synopsis, and meta tags – are effectively integrated into your metadata, they form a powerful marketing tool that maximizes the discoverability of your book. Each component plays a unique role in attracting and engaging potential readers, ultimately driving sales and expanding your audience reach.

In the competitive landscape of self-publishing, optimizing metadata is not just important; it's essential. It enables authors to cut through the clutter and connect with their target audience in a meaningful way. By investing time and effort into crafting metadata that accurately represents your book and appeals to your target readership, you lay a solid foundation for success in the ever-evolving world of publishing.

Chapter 16

"REUP" THE SCIENCE OF GETTING YOUR BOOK NOTICED.

Here we go y'all, now is the time for us to dive into the publicity aspect of marketing. As we've stated in the past, marketing is the entire process of a books creation, publishing, and publicity. Everything from the type of story you write, to the title/cover/ and layout, to the metadata, to the manner in which you publish AS WELL AS who you publish through, and finally the never-ending process of publicity campaign marketing. Every bit of that is marketing.

Before we move on, you need to check yourself in case you skipped over Part 2, because you will wreck yourself. Everything me an Geo laid out for you in those chapters is of the utmost importance. Their not suggestions, they are science of book success. And their being laid down to you by a true self made man in the prison publishing industry. If you don't know who George Kayer is by this point, crawl out from under your rock, put away your pride, and let that man school you up.

The number one thing you need to remember about the publicity campaign aspect of marketing, is that there ain't no such thing as to much campaign marketing. And it never ends. You have to campaign each book you publish nonstop if you want to continually generate an average annual sales statistic. Just like on the streets, there's always some hoochy looking to make a move on your man, always some youngsters after your territory.

There's a good chance your manuscript is already finished, so you may think the science in Part 2 is unnecessary, but its not. You will eventually write more books, or do a Relaunch Tune Up mentioned in it Is Never To Late. Trust me, this will become an addiction to you. And, the more books you publish, the more royalties you'll make every year. It is quite possible for you to earn 5 figures a year from prison as an author. But it ain't gonna happen unless you fully embrace Geo's methodology of Whole Book Marketing. So do yourself a favor, if you skipped part one or two go read them.

For this next part, Geo and I will begin to school you in the science of publicity marketing, and how the professionals at Cadmus will see your vision into a reality, as we'll as school you up on how to take direct part in your books publicity right from your prison cell.

Finally before we begin, understand the concept that nothing in this world is free. Publicity Campaign Marketing costs money, and your gonna have to spend some to make your book a big success. Even the free publicity campaign stuff is gonna cost you money, because last time I checked stamps and prepaid calls ain't free.

GEORGE R. KAYER AND VINNIE VALE

"PENPIMPING"

The pen is mightier than the sword. Ain't that how the saying goes? Well its true. Your most obvious option for assisting your marketing campaign as an imprisoned person is letter writing, or as we like to call it PenPimping. This means getting your grind on by mailing out hand written letters to cats that are capable of bringing peeps awareness to your book. A.K.A, pimping out your book player!

You can try and write letters to folks like Kim Kardashian who could recommend your book to her millions of social media followers, but that's not very realistic now is it? But let's say you reach out to someone who can recommend your book to hundreds of cats? Let's go even further and say you've reached out to a dozen people that can do that, now you've turned those hundreds of people into thousands of people. Are you catching what I'm dropping here? Instead of shooting your harpoon at a whale, try and snag a few dozen salmon.

There is the chance you've become something like Charles Manson, and have garnered infamy for your criminal exploits, which will give the rarified ability to catch the attention of said whale. In that case, shoot your shot. But for the rest of us "average joe" crooks, we gotta get our PenPimping on. The more letters you write, the better.

"But who should I write?" Well, that's the best part. EVERYONE! The potential is endless. We've given you the example of writing to podcasts you find on your tablet, but there's also the possibility of writing to various prison institutions across the country to request they recommended your book to their population. Prison libraries Buy books yo! Geo said he has had the most success writing other authors and researchers. They are a curious group and you are the novelty.

You can also reach out to all your family, friends, old coworkers, bosses, teachers, hell even your former attorneys/prosecutors/judges. None of those people may even have use for the type of book your publishing, but it is more about putting the word out through them that you have published a book. They all have social media I'm sure, that right their is word of mouth publicity (which we will cover more in our next chapter).

Other places you can personally write are libraries located in your state, as well as local mom and pop book shops. Provide both places with your ISBN number automatically just in case their interested. You can also personally contact prisoner focused book stores like Books N Things, Sureshot, and Freebird Publishers to request they sell your book. If you published with Cadmus your book is available wholesale for retailers to purchase through Ingram or Cadmus Publishing.

Anyways, the possibilities of PenPimping your book are endless. Most of the big contacts I recommended like and Books N Things will be taken care of through Cadmus with the press release, but it can never hurt for you to personally contact them as well. But, we think you got the most of the PenPimping concept, so let's move on to Word Of Mouth.

(See the list of organizations you can PenPimp in the Appendix)

WORD OF MOUTH, AIN'T WHAT IT USED TO BE, OR IS IT?
George here,

If you are reading this in prison you know the value of ROY, Rumors On The Yard, ie., word of mouth.. It is literally how we find out everything we need to know to survive and thrive, like what rules have changed, usually for the worse. The concept of word of mouth hasn't changed for 50,000 years and it is still the best, free marketing any author or business can implement but, to use any human nature to ones advantage you have to know the science, how does it work, why it doesn't work.

The fact is, you already know how word of mouth works and why it works. It is a primary tool for humans to exchange information and those who engage in this social behavior are more socially and factually informed than the rest of us.

Why it works: Think about it the next time someone walks up to you and tells you something, anything. Think about the emotions the message brings to the surface, is it ho hum, no body I know cares about that or is it a Oh Shit, I gotta go tell my husband and Billy Bob right now? Word of mouth works ONLY when the message means something to the person hearing it or reading it in their news feed or someone they know who is interested in that message.

How it works:
The why and how word of mouth works are intrinsically linked yet separate, here's why. How it works is one person sharing information with another person. Why it works is only because the information being shared is relevant to the person or people they know. As an entrepreneur, an author it is your job to have a word-of-mouth plan whether you do it yourself or hire a professional marketing team.

At Cadmus it is my job to have a word-of-mouth plan not just for the company but to promote all Cadmus authors. And it may surprise you, and don't tell Vinnie because he thinks I know everything and I'd like to keep it that way. But, when it comes to the digital word of mouth world, all I know are the basics. I can thrive knowing only the basics because we employ a digital word of mouth marketing company, it is what they specialize in. They are experts in finding people who want to hear our message, or your message and you know what that audience is called, its called potential buyers, and they find them by the tens of thousands. That's the how side of the digital word of mouth plan.

WHO DOESN'T ENJOY A DAMN GOOD ARTICLE?

George here,
Writing and submitting articles to magazines is one of the best ways authors can capitalize on free word of mouth yet, with the digital world, people in prisons are excluded from this source of free promotion. Until Now. The only thing to exceed the joy of seeing your book in print is seeing your writing in a major magazine. I know the feeling, I was first published in the NRA's magazine, The American Rifleman..... at age 14. The joy is the same with each successive article however, I stopped writing for magazines once Inmate Shopper took off and it became a full-time business.

I'm so excited to announce that Cadmus is creating, in addition to the new Books By Prisoners website an Articles By Prisoners platform where magazine editors my come read your articles and purchase them. This solves the problems and challenges of submitting your article from prison. The service is free, for more details see the back of the book. Okay, back to Vinnie.

   No publication company, be it newspaper, magazine, or website relies entirely on in house writers for articles. A good portion of what they produce is written by freelancers. These are cats that work as independent writers who submits their work to the various companies out there to be published in their periodicals or on their websites. For their work, they are paid fees as freelance authors.

   Now, you consider yourself to be a writer obviously. You've written at least one book, and we're sure you've written many essays and the like throughout your life. Why can't you be a freelance writer? It is a fantastic way to get your name out there, as well as develop your skills and I.Q as a writer.

   What periodicals do you submit to you ask? Well that's a broad spectrum, but let's start with what your current book is about. Is your book a memoir, well how about submitting stories to The Moth, The Sun, or any other periodical that covers life experience? Is it a Jail House Lawyer book? How about writing an article for Prison Legal.

   You wrote a book on Wicca or Paganism you say? OK that's easy, submit articles to Witches And Pagans. Oh, your super cold with it and busted out a real inventive SciFi thriller? Submit stories to Asimov's Science Fiction. Like we said, the options are endless. You don't even have to write articles that relate tour book(s). Places like Mother Jones are always looking for commentary written on prison life by prisoners, especially if its covering the corruption or hypocrisies conducted by the institutions administration and staff.

   The way you go about submitting queries to these companies will vary from place to place. Usually they want you to follow specific guidelines for submissions that may sound intimidating at first, but really aren't. These guidelines are traditionally done one one page, single spaced and usually involve the following

   + your contact info
   + a short greeting to the editor
   + a short paragraph that summarizes the intended article
   + a short paragraph giving the editor an idea of the works

structure and content

+ a short paragraph explaining your expertise in the subject matter of your submission

+ a short thank you and sign off.

Most magazines/newspapers/websites want you to include the prewritten article with your query. There's a lot of work that goes into this process. Once again it may seem intimidating at first, but like we said its not.

And some of these places pay really well. Mother Jones for example accepts submissions anywhere from 500-5,000 words, and pays $1 a word. There is an entire side hustle available to convict authors by way of freelancing. Its not just a way to get your name out there, but also a way to load up your inmate bank account with dead presidents.

Chapter 17

SMALL BUDGET ADVERTISING

Beta Test:
"Shooting your shot with online advertising"

Geo here,
This is where the big dogs play and the little dogs like us have an equal shot if you know the game. If you hit me up and ask Cadmus to run Google ads for you, without the proper beta testing, I won't do it. I'm not your guy. Unless you do the beta test and build a custom audience you are flushing your ad dollars down the crapper. That means no sales and who ya going to blame, not ya momma, Cadmus.

What do I mean by a custom audience? This is the cool part, our marketing department looks at, not reads, your book, picks out the genre, sub genres, then does some kind of nerd magic to develop a psychological profile of those people.. What they like, where they hang out, what keywords make them stop and read your ad. Then they create a few test ads, run those test ads in front of a few hundred thousand viewers and see how well they preform, how many times people click on them. This is the same shit billion-dollar corporations do before launching their ad campaigns, why? BECAUSE IT WORKS.

Does this beta test guarantee sales? That's not the right question. The question is: what do I learn from the beta test? You learn from the people who should be interested in your product if they ARE interested. Exactly how many of those 100,000 viewers clicked on your ad to look at your book, if your book is on Cadmus we can tell you how long each person looked at your pages, and if they bought your book.

You learn that if 20,000 clicked on your ad but spend only a few seconds on your page, it is a good indication your book cover is a turn off. If they spend a minute or more on your page but don't buy it tells us the price may be too high. Or they wanted an eBook and you didn't offer one. And if you get lucky, maybe a few visitors will leave a message and tell you what they think.

After the first beta test we usually make adjustments based on what we learned then run another test and see if we get better results. The second test is usually half the cost of the first test because much of the work has already been done.

What about Youtube and Tiktok, I want my books advertised there. We can do that. Understand those platforms are a whole different animal then a simple text ad on a news feed. The testing is much more expensive because it's video baby. There are additional cost associated with actors, getting 1 copy or 20 copies of your book or t-shirts to the actor to use as promotion.. Someone has to write the dialogue for the actor and tell them to be serious, happy, sad, read from the book, wear the T-shirt and on and on.

Here's Vinnie with some numbers. Internet advertising is huge. As huge as Precious and Moniques appetites combined. Your gonna hit tens of millions of eyeballs in your career as a writer just through online advertisements. And their way cheaper than print ads. As it was stated in the previous chapter, 80% of book searches begin on Amazon. I can only imagine the kind of numbers Google generates.

Yes, there is the fact that when it comes to marketing, more people seeing your ads does not equate to more sales. Why is that? Simple.

Think of the cats you hang with, how many like Barbie dolls, hopefully zero, but there's nothing wrong with that if this is what your into. My point is, no matter the product, a book a song a magazine, the ad must be shown to the someone who has an interest or it is ignored, isn't it.

Internet surfing moves way too fast, and it causes way too much of an eyegasm for the ad to even register with a quarter of the people that will end up seeing it. But let's get a little hypothetical going. Say 100,000 people see your ad every seven days. That's 25,000 people a week that may show interest in your ad. Let's say you sell to .1% of them.... that's 25 books a week just from that add. Those 25 books a week turn into 1,300 books a year. Now how about them numbers? I don't know if your aware of this, but an author usually makes about 20% of the cover price, so let's say your book is priced at $20, which means you get about $4 a book. $4 a book times 1,300 is $5,200 a year. That's just one book, and one well placed ad running daily.

We here at Cadmus excel in the online marketing game. So we got you covered with nukes on this front of the battle plan.

Chapter 18

AFFORDABLE ALTERNATIVES TO AN AD CAMPAIGN.

These activities listed here really should be done before most ad campaigns but are also effective stand alone Branding activities recommended by A Marketing Expert dot com. They are international book marketing and media relations experts.

Listicles:
Listicles are the genre of list and quizzes. You've seen them in your favorite magazines and on the news, especially during holidays.
 Listicles are an inexpensive way to draw attention to any platform you may be using.? And if your list or quiz is really interesting, it's not hard to see it placed / shared on other sites like Buzzfeed. And of course it contains a link back to your site or your book on Cadmus.

Gift Guides:
Are another tool for your branding toolbox. Also gift guides aren't just for holidays they are year-round, so they can stay on your to-do list. What about a gift guide for prisoners? or prisoners' families?

Local libraries.
You may be surprised, local libraries love local authors. If you are not hated by the local populace we recommend you invest some thought and time into some local branding. Perhaps a friend or family member can drop in with a copy of your book or, if you are a Cadmus author you can arrange for us to send the

librarian a copy with your letter.

Local Influencers.
Local media may feel less glamorous than going viral on a national platform but remember, all press is good press. And like libraries, local media loves their local authors. Don't forget local bookstores (yes, Cadmus will process wholesale orders for you) and specialty shops related to your book.

Blogs.
Blogs are the 'Getting to know you' aspect of an authors branding and an awesome way to communicate to or with new readers. Blogs serve as a tool for creating a multidimensional brand with insider information, deep dives into characters, yours or other authors who have influenced you. Its a chance to expand your story line, share an alternative ending to one's storyline.

Podcast.
Podcast listeners have increased by 40 million just last year. That's around 20% of all internet users. It seems everyone is listening to at least one. I listen to a few on my tablet as well. If you love to hear yourself talk, consider writing out a loose script of ideas, run through it a few times then have someone record it and post it on your social or other open podcast platforms. We at Cadmus are considering how we can add this service for our authors in 2024.

For non fiction authors blogs are a way to show you stay apprised on current topics and remain a thought leader in the genre.

Now consider these numbers about an ad campaigns. shelf life.
Ads are not saved by search engines, when your ad budget is spent they disappear. Here are some average lengths of time (shelf life) your post will will be relevant on big name platforms:

Tiktok: within minutes unless shared.

X: 18 minutes.
Fb\meta: 5 hours.
Instagram: 21 hours.
LinkedIn: 24 hours.

  Now consider the options we just covered, all have potential to be viewed or listened to for months depending on the platform used.

Chapter 19

SOCIAL MEDIA = SOCIAL MONEY.

As everyone who doesn't live under a rock on Mars knows: social media is king in the marketing world nowadays. If you ain't poppin on the "Gram" or any other platform, your "street cred" dips a few notches. All your peeps have a social media pressence, including grandma and grandpa. Well, maybe not everyone. I doubt Osama Bin Laden was cruising around MySpace or Facebook, but who knows. The fact is though, anyone who owns a company (in your your case, you are the "company") needs to be poppin on social media. So you most definitely need to be up on the social media game.

When I was a 20 year old peewee peckerwood coming up on the yard, an old schooler who was almost 2 decades older than me, (but still only a few notches above me in the pecking order), put me up on some game that he said he learned to late. He told me that the point to putting in work is more about keeping your name relevant to the rest of the population throughout the state, especially to the powers that be who are slammed down in supermax as well as their mouthpieces on the yards who run shit for them. He said that you can go and stab one of the names in the hat to death, and you'll be respected and relevant for a handful of years. But you need to continue that momentum, you need to maintain that publicity, you need to keep your name in the forefront of peoples minds. I did all that he told me, and by my late 20's I was one of the mouthpieces running shit for the guys in supermax. On my way to becoming one of them. I was also getting ready to begin my death sentence, so thanks for the advice asshole.

    Anyways, the point is you need to keep yourself and your books in the publics eye. That's the laymen's Confuscious saying for all advertising, especially social media. That shit moves at such a lighting pace, that you need to be the hare and not the tortoise. Its also hella cheaper than any other form of publicity marketing. But you need to keep pimpin that bitch. An idle Facebook or X account is worthless. You need to post up on them continuously. Just having an account ain't enough, you need to draw attention to it. Just like your book, if no one knows it exists, its just a paperweight.

    We would suggest building a dedicated social media presence as an author separate from any personal one you may already have. You're building a brand here, not trying hook back up with a long-lost crush from high school. On Fb, this done like a business page, where people can "follow" you instead of you "friending" peeps. This also allows people to "like" your page, which will automatically set them as a person "following" you, allowing them to see all of your posts.

    The type of content you should post is anything that builds your brand as an author and writer. Anything that can draw interest in your work. This is not a place to post your fringe political views (unless that's what you write books about), or old photos from your families trip to Disneyland when you were 12. Post about your career as an author and other things pertaining to it

    At this point your probably asking yourself, "how am I suppose to do all this from prison Vinnie?!?!?" Well, once again Cadmus got you player! We will create, run, and maintain any social media accounts you want. We will even piggy back the comments and content posted back and forth with you. You will be able to post personally on your social media through us, and we will post AS YOU on your social media accounts. We got you covered, yet again. Your welcome (yet again) :)

    Geo here,
What's all this cost you're wondering?
    After you do the Beta testing to see if anyone cares about your book and presuming the test indicated an ad campaign would be

profitable.

You should figure a minimum of $80 per month on ads which is cool if that spend is bringing in a hundred or two hundred. Then you can peel off some to increase your social footprint and direct that traffic to your bookstore. Are ya beginning to see the big picture?

Chapter 20

"THE SLOW LONESOME DEATH OF PRINT ADS"

George here,
Print ads are slowly going the way of the dinosaurs, CD's and humans? Once upon a time they ruled the publishing industry like the T-Rex. But over the last decade and a half, the print industry has been making the transition to news feeds, blogs and eZines (Internet Magazines/Newspapers).

There are always exceptions:
For those of us who's demographic is people in prison, non fiction, self help or resource books, ads in prisoner publications can be profitable. But, they are only a slice of the pie, we want to eat the whole pie.

Nearly 80% of book searches nowadays begin on Amazon. The need to spend buckets of money advertising in print ads has become unpopular for good reasons, no analytics and its ridiculously expensive. Not long ago I read an article in Publisher Magazine on the advantages of digital ads. One powerful publisher was very candid, stating: the only reason I run a big ad in New York Times or USA Today is when I scoop another publisher's star writer and want to rub their nose in it.

And this brings me to my final point, the psychology of your ad. I see ya scratching your head, wondering what this fool be about?

Here's a personal example: when I considered the ad campaign for Cadmus, I knew it had to begin with a "Statement! Ad" in Prison Legal News. A Statement Ad is just that, its not a nice ad on any old page, like our competition. A statement ad is the best designed ad, the biggest ad, and on the most expensive page in the publication. Sure, potential customers can't miss it but the statement part of the ad is making a statement to the competition. Our ad on the back cover of Prison Legal News tells the competitors there's a new Lead Dog on the yard and we're making it rain MF.

Okay, back to Vinnie.

Peep this skullduggery... It cost $31,000 to run a 1/16th page ad in the USA Today... for one day. ONE DAY! YOU GOTTA BE FUCKIN KIDDING ME?!?!? I understand that millions of cats read that newspaper, but what kind of author has that kinda money to blow? Stephen king, that's who. Millionaires.

But, allow me to play Devils Advocate for a second. Print ads are not completely useless for us, especially when the print ads are convict specific publications such as Prison Legal News, etc. Sometimes the cats your trying catch the attention of can be reached relatively easy through print ads. Specialty topics for example like Witchcraft/Paganism. Magazines like Witches And Pagans, or PanGaia are great places to advertise your book, and last time I checked it only costs $20 for 20 words, and $0.75 per word after the 20. That's a fast, cheap, and simple way to bring attention to a large number of potential buyers.

Most authors nowadays skip past print ad marketing. They do take a long time to show up (called lead time) in the publications. They are also expensive, and most people have switched over to the digital copies of their favorite periodicals (magazines/newspapers). This drastically cuts down on the number of eyeballs that could potentially see your ad.

At the end of the day I, Vinnie, give the Roman Emperors thumbs down on print ad marketing. But let's hear what Old Skewl Geo has to say about it?

(I concur.)

Chapter 21

SO YOU WANT AN AUTHOR'S WEBSITE

    The purpose for an author having a website is so that their footprint is even larger in the world community. You can use it as a place for you to post news updates about future book releases, to sell your already released books, to post blogs, to post your bio as an author, and to give your contact information. I mean hell, you can use it for whatever you want as long as it pertains to your career as an author. You can even set it up with advertising so that you generate profits from traffic, if you wanted to be "that guy". Its just another one of the tools an author has that says to the world "I Am Here".

    Having a website gives you more flexibility than a standard social media page. You can only post so many characters in a social media post. A website blog offers the chance to put up a longer, more in depth stream of thought. A webpage and social media page differ greatly in many ways. They're both very useful, and very important in their own rights. And you can run links back and forth between your social media pages and website.

    The whole purpose to all this once again, is to promote your book and yourself.

    Thanks for the rosy glasses look at websites Vinnie.
    Geo here, you've heard the saying: if only I knew then what I know now.
    That sums up my experiences with web sites and why one of my first projects at Cadmus was to build Books by Prisoners

SELL YOUR BOOKS FROM PRISON

Interactive Bookstore. An affordable alternative to expensive websites. Even if you are lucky enough to have a loved one experienced in web design, its not enough. Do you have a credit card, all web host require one. Do you have a bank account for Shopify to make deposits into? How will you drive traffic to your site? That requires SEO and near constant social media marketing. I learned all this the hard way, the expensive way and spent thousands learning what doesn't work and why.

    Most folks can't afford to pay professionals to set up their website, its expensive. Here are some average recommended hourly rates from Writers Market:
Blogging, $59 per hour.
SEO, $57. per hour.
Press releases, $85. per hour.
Writing content for websites, $48. per hour.
Video scripts for ads on You Tube, TlkTok, $77. per hour.
Social media management, $57. per hour
Copy Editing, $51. per hour.
Web design, $65. per hour.

    Then, say your significant other sets up your website and social media, then you breakup. Even if you have the login info and password we can't get in unless your x partner sends us the 3rd party verification code within minutes of our attempted login.

    Amazon profile pages are a huge advantage for authors if you have someone who can get access to it. But if they bail on you you are screwed. And, we just received notice that Amazon no longer allows you to place links on your page. (Dec. 2023)
    For all these reasons and more I created an affordable bookstore platform for people in prison. One that will be there long after your current helpers have disappeared. Here are some of the advantages of a Books by Prisoners bookstore:

    * Of course, sell your book(s) with Shopify.
    * Sell your book swag, t-shirts, caps mugs with the book title.
    * post short stories.
    * post art.

* post photo and about the author,
* links to your social media, blogs, video, music, pen pal site.
* Visitors can leave a message or email you.
* Forward your website address to your bookstore.
* Obtain a matching email to your website.
* You can do everything in your bookstore that you can do with an expensive website and Cadmus will be there to manage it for you.

Plus, we advertise the Books by Prisoners platform on Instagram, X, Fb, Threads YouTube, TikTok and LinkedIn to drive traffic to the site.

Any ad campaigns you run can drop customers right on your personal landing page, they see all your stuff first.

Not only that we can tell you how many visitors you had, how long they stayed and more.

Mic drop.

More About Websites: by AI, ChatGPT

10 Most Important Tasks Associated with Setting Up a Business Website:

1. **Define Objectives:** Clearly outline the purpose and goals of your website, whether it's e-commerce, lead generation, brand awareness, etc.

2. **Choose a Domain Name:** Select a memorable and relevant domain name that reflects your brand identity.

3. **Select a Web Hosting Provider:** Choose a reliable web hosting service that meets your website's needs in terms of speed, reliability, and scalability.

4. **Design and Development:** Create a visually appealing and user-friendly website design, ensuring it's responsive across all devices.

5. **Content Creation:** Develop high-quality content that

engages your target audience and aligns with your brand messaging.

6. **SEO Optimization:** Implement on-page and off-page SEO strategies to improve your website's visibility in search engine results.

7. **Integrate Analytics:** Set up analytics tools like Google Analytics to track website traffic, user behavior, and performance metrics.

8. **Security Measures:** Install security plugins, SSL certificates, and other measures to protect your website from cyber threats and ensure customer data security.

9. **Testing and Optimization:** Conduct thorough testing to identify and fix any issues, optimize website speed, and improve user experience.

10. **Launch and Promotion:** Once everything is ready, officially launch your website and promote it through various channels like social media, email marketing, and online advertising.

8 Most Common Expenses Incurred:

1. **Domain Registration:** Cost associated with registering a domain name for your website.

2. **Web Hosting:** Charges for hosting your website on a server, typically on a monthly or annual basis.

3. **Website Design and Development:** Fees for hiring professionals or purchasing website templates for design and development.

4. **Content Creation:** Expenses related to creating high-quality content including text, images, videos, and graphics.

5. **SEO Services:** Cost for hiring SEO experts or investing

in SEO tools and services to optimize your website for search engines.

   6. **Security Measures:** Expenditure on security plugins, SSL certificates, and other measures to protect your website from cyber threats.

   7. **Marketing and Advertising:** Budget allocated for promoting your website through various online channels such as social media ads, PPC campaigns, and influencer marketing.

   8. **Maintenance and Updates:** Funds required for ongoing maintenance, updates, and technical support to keep your website running smoothly and up-to-date with the latest technologies and trends.

   10 Most Important Tasks Associated with Setting Up a Shopify Business Website:

   1. **Sign Up and Account Setup:** Register for a Shopify account and complete initial setup including store name, address, and currency.

   2. **Choose a Theme:** Browse and select a suitable theme from Shopify's theme store or customize one according to your brand's aesthetics and requirements.

   3. **Product Upload and Management:** Add products to your Shopify store, including images, descriptions, prices, and inventory management.

   4. **Payment Gateway Integration:** Set up payment gateways to accept online payments securely, considering options like Shopify Payments, PayPal, or third-party providers.

   5. **Customization and Branding:** Customize your Shopify store to reflect your brand identity through logo placement, color schemes, fonts, and other branding elements.

6. **SEO Optimization:** Optimize product descriptions, meta tags, and other on-page elements for better visibility in search engine results.

7. **Apps and Extensions Integration:** Explore and install relevant Shopify apps and extensions to enhance functionality, such as email marketing, live chat, and social media integration.

8. **Shipping Setup:** Configure shipping rates, options, and carriers to ensure smooth order fulfillment and delivery processes.

9. **Launch and Testing:** Test your website thoroughly to ensure functionality, usability, and compatibility across devices before officially launching it to the public.

10. **Marketing and Promotion:** Develop a marketing strategy to drive traffic to your Shopify store, including social media marketing, email campaigns, content marketing, and other promotional efforts.

8 Most Common Expenses Incurred:

1. **Monthly Subscription Fee:** Regular subscription fee charged by Shopify for using its platform, varying based on the chosen plan.

2. **Transaction Fees:** Charges incurred for processing online payments through Shopify Payments or other payment gateways, typically a percentage of each transaction or a flat fee.

3. **Theme Purchase or Customization:** Cost associated with purchasing premium themes from the Shopify theme store or hiring developers/designers for custom theme customization.

4. **App Fees:** Expenses for installing and using third-party Shopify apps and extensions to add additional functionalities to your store.

5. **Product Photography:** Investment in professional product photography services to showcase products effectively on your Shopify store.

6. **Marketing and Advertising:** Budget allocated for marketing campaigns, including social media ads, Google Ads, influencer collaborations, and other promotional activities to drive traffic and sales.

7. **Shipping Costs:** Expenditure related to shipping products to customers, including packaging materials, postage fees, and shipping carrier charges.

8. **Customer Support and Services:** Funds allocated for providing excellent customer support, including hiring support staff, implementing live chat services, or outsourcing customer service operations.

Chapter 22

BOOK REVIEWERS, BLURBS, PRESS RELEASES.

I gotta step on Vinnie's toes here to make a clarification. Book reviews are not blurbs, but blurbs (in today's digital age) are now considered reviews. It's important as a writer, author to know the difference. One cost hundreds of dollars while the other one is often free.

The formal book review is expensive and requires time, it is an actual professional reviewer who reads some or all of your book and writes a 100 to 500 word review, good or bad. Then they publish their review on their platform or magazine. Just because you pay a reviewer doesn't mean the reviewer will tell his readers your book is great, if it isn't. A credible reviewer isn't going to lie about your book and risk their reputation for a few hundred dollars.

Blurb reviews sell books. Look at the back cover of this book then look at the first few pages in the front of the book. Now ask yourself a simple question: I'm looking at two books on the same topic, one book has no blurb reviews, the other book, like this one, has pages of excellent blurb reviews. Which one will you buy? We already know the answer.

Okay Vinnie they all yours.
When cats are perusing their preferred online retailer for books, they always wanna see what other folks have to say about their potential choices. If what their scoping out ain't got no reviews, they may very likely bypass it. So, any kind of positive

reviews you can get are important. Remember though, reviews alone don't help market your books, you have to get the cats who are shopping to notice it first. The review acts as a tool to "convince" them to buy the book.

Some authors see reviews as being ATM machines. But how do you generate them? You could do the method of "you scratch my back, and I'll scratch yours" with other authors. This method is when two or more authors agree to read each other's books and give honest, though slanted towards positive reviews of one another's books. But then there is a credibility issue, only well-known professional reviewers are recognized by the literary community. You can inspire your family and friends on the streets to leave reviews on Amazon, etc., bit these again are not "reviews". You can also generate them organically, though its few and far between. You may get one review posted every 100 books sold organically. One of the best ways to garner free reviews is when anytime you chop it up with someone concerning your book, you encourage them to not just read your book, but to leave a blurb review as well.

There's also Book Bloggers. These cats make their living as online influencers through blog sites and other social media, whose platform of topics and discussions surround the publishing industry. Specifically reviewing books (etc.), discussing up coming releases, gossiping on news within the industry itself, and doing interviews with authors, editors, and others from within the industry. They are a huge source for any author or editor to have in their Network.

Cadmus offers you reader review services that are legitimate, and not falsified. We also have an entire Rolodex of Book Bloggers and other influencers that will work with for you. And a blurb club for blurbs.

Chapter 23

PRESS RELEASE? WHY SHOULD I CARE?

What is a press release you ask?

Well, a press release or (PR) is a short, but detailed write up about you and your book that is sent out to hundreds or thousands of various media outlets, (websites, newspapers, news feeds, magazines, TV and radio) to bring attention to you and your work. It says to the publishing industry "I Am Here".

Below is the actual press release sent out by Cadmus Publishing after being acquired by George and Ken.

MEDIA RELEASE: Oct 15, 2023

Death Row Inmate Acquires Cadmus Publishing

One of America's most published prisoners and a reentry citizen acquires Cadmus Publishing, the number one publishing services company for people in prisons. George Kayer was first published by the National Rifle Association at age 14, then struggled with undiagnosed dyslexia and bipolar conditions for decades. Convicted of first-degree murder and sentenced to death in 1993. In early 2000, Kayer was inspired by a pen pal, Author Nancy Mairs. Mairs encouraged Kayer to begin writing again and since has spent the last 20+ years helping inmates connect with critical services listed in his books for prisoners: resource guides like Offline Shopper and Snail Mail Pen paling, information previously unavailable to prisoners.

"I have tried to honor the death of my victim by giving back to others," Kayer said. "A lot of state prisons tout rehabilitation but in reality, discourage, even punish artists and writers for trying to market their intellectual property. I am thankful Arizona has codified prisoners' rights in these areas. Prison administrators from complex Warden Ibarra to my counselor, COIII Freeland have been exceptional in the free flow of information, a primary requirement for a writer. Arizona prison policies should be considered by other states' prisons rather than administrators crushing a person's creativity and desire to repay society."

Kayer is joined by his partner on the street, Kenny Passaro, owner of Prison Living Press. Passaro, like many people after release from prison, struggled for years. Passaro credits his turnaround to getting off prison psych meds and getting on Jesus. The two entrepreneurs have known each other for the past decade. Passaro said, "This is an amazing opportunity to serve God and to continue serving the needs, desires, and dreams of the talented people in prisons."

Katie Cruz, Media Relations
admin@cadmuspublishing.com

You can write your own press release and distribute it, but it is actually very difficult for a layperson and for someone to do in our situation. This is one of those jobs better done by a pro with access to keyword optimization. That's where Cadmus once again comes in. They basically have their own PR dept.

Geo here, writing a press release has become a complicated technological mess, from my point of view. It use to be simple: George did this or that, run it in the town newspaper and everybody new about it. Now days it's all about SEO, audience targeting and the keywords needed to do it. It also depends on what's happening in the news cycle.

The week Cadmus was scheduled to do our release, fricken Hamas invaded Israel and Israel was planning their invasion. We did the release before Israel invaded but the major media was already distracted, preparing their newsrooms to cover this critical story.

SELL YOUR BOOKS FROM PRISON

We still got traction from Fox and some other media platforms and, nearly doubled our web traffic but it could have been better. My best result was an article I wrote about toilet paper, or the lack thereof in prison.. It was picked up by 92 media platforms including all the majors.

Why you should care about press releases?
If you care at all about repairing your image on the internet, press releases are your friend. If you Google me, there are five or more pages of results about all my books and stuff I've written. There's so much content one has to look carefully to even notice I'm in prison.

This is called Cleaning Up your Footprint. If you have an out date I encourage you to do some press releases, they are the first things a potential employer will see when they Google you. Not to mention potential readers.

Making your press release stand out.
This is where you want to use your incarceration to your advantage.

Notice in the Cadmus press release, the first words are: Death Row Prisoner. This was no mistake, 'death row' has more Google searches than George Kayer. Every sentence is a mathematical calculation of SEO and keywords and why you should never write your own press release.. Unless your a trained digital marketer or IT person.

Why use your real name or own that your a prisoner? Because it's a big deal when a prisoner writes a book compared to the one million people who publish books every year. Look at these two headlines:

Mary Jane releases Baking Cookies book.
Arizona Prisoner Writes How to Make Cookies in Prison.
One is more interesting than the other.
Your competition is using all the tricks they can, you should too.

Mary Jane's book would never draw the interest of the Criminal Justice book buyers but the Headline: Arizona Prisoner Writes..... now that opens your book up to a whole market not available to others.

GEORGE R. KAYER AND VINNIE VALE

If you have a title of interest to prisoners or criminal justice, Cadmus has a press release service that reaches 50+ magazines, journals and newsletters in the criminal justice genre. Again, it's all about getting your message in front of those who want to hear your message.

Chapter 24

BRICK AND MORTAR BOOKSTORES

The golden goose of any author is to see their books on the shelf at a big ass brick and mortar publishing company like Barnes and Noble. Its a worthy goal, and we understand the allure of it, but to be honest with you... its unreasonable. Sorry. That's not saying its IMPOSSIBLE, its just IMPROBABLE unless your book goes viral.

You see, the problem with big brick and mortar bookstores is a little thing invented by the Devil called "bureaucracy". Barnes and Noble is a billion dollar corporation, and as such has a complex hierarchy of employees and executives. You could contact your local B and N, and try to request they order and stock your books on their shelves, but that decision is being made by people that those cats you'd be talking to have never met or heard of. Even if one of your loved ones is a the manager of a local B and N, you still wouldn't get your shit put on their shelves.

Now, on the other hand, being shelved at small mom and pop bookstores is absolutely obtainable. Especially if they are in the state your from, grew up in, or where your currently residing. In fact, most local mom and pop shops have an entire section dedicated solely to authors from their turf. And, the people who decide which books go on the shelves in these stores WORK AT THE STORES. That means they are easily reachable for petitions requesting to shelve your book(s).

So, how do you go about requesting these small local brick

and mortars order and stock your books on their shelves? Well that's easy, you just fuckin do it. In fact, we'll do it for you. You can make a list out of all the local independent bookstores in your city/town, or even state, and we at Cadmus will contact them to request they carry your book. I know, we're awesome. Your welcome. We'll also work with you on pricing for brick and mortar bookstores because the stores themselves usually like to make about 40% of the cover price. We have a contract with Ingram Spark printers and can easily meet the orders of a small brick and mortar stores if need be. And we know the best pricing scale for you to "shelf price" your book. That way you make a decent profit after everyone gets into your pocket. Also, another brick and mortar option is libraries, and we at Cadmus will take care of that if you so desire. Ask for pricing and FAQs.

But, at the end of the day, internet is king. You will be "on the shelf" in thousands of online stores on the planet. You will be "on the shelf" of Amazon. And you will be "on the shelf" in hundreds of other (albeit smaller) internet bookstores on the internet. So cheer up.

Lastly, if you get rejected by a store, don't cry about it. Rejection and publishing go hand in hand, like a wino and a 40oz. If you can't deal with rejection OR criticism, find a another career. You are not going to last in this one.

(I just love it when Vinnie's so cheerful).

Chapter 25

KEEPING A STASH SPOT OF BOOKS

Rejoice, for its the dawn of a new day! That is because the publishing industry currently lives in the age of P.O.D (Print On Demand). This means when a book is ordered on the internet, it is printed from a digital file saved in storage on a computer system. So, gone are the days of having to prepay for, and then store in your garage 1,000+ books. Happy times!

Now that's not to say you shouldn't have a few copies of your book handy. Who knows, you may find someone on your cell block that's interested in what you have to offer. This way you'll be able to trade them in commissary on the spot. This is good for you, cause it'll be money straight onto your pocket due to the fact that there wont be any retailers, etc., putting their hands in your pocket. And its good for the buyer because they won't have to pay the shipping cost or wait for delivery. Your also eliminating the possibility of these potential customers forgetting to order your book at a later time from a retailer. Or even worse, having second thoughts about spending their money on your book.

There's also the campaign marketing tactic of promotion. This tactic includes many battle plans, but one such option is the hustle of sending your book to internet influencers for free with the hopes that they will review and recommend it. Well guess what, we at Cadmus got you covered there. We not only have influential book bloggers that we work with, we will also send out up to

4 free digital copies to sources that you tell us about.

    Geo here, Don't forget to send copies to the governor, prison director and warden.
    Another advantage of having books on hand is this is the only way for your readers to get autographed copies of your book. I've sold dozens of books because the book came autographed from prison. Readers get a thrill out of having an autographed copy from a prisoner. And they're willing to pay for it. Now, while most prisons don't allow us to process orders from prison, if your a Cadmus author, customers may send us the payments and you can mail them the book from prison, too cool!!

Chapter 26

WHY SHOULD I WRITE A SECOND BOOK ?
MOMENTUM.

The science of momentum might just be the most valuable lesson in this whole book. Why is that you ask? Because Geo and I are about to flip your grams into ounces, and your ounces into bank, ya dig?

Think about this logic...Even before you finish the book, how many people have you told about it? Old school word of mouth in action.

When you finish reading a good book, do you simply throw it to the way side, or do you stop and think, "I wonder if this author has anything else available?"

That question right there is one that 90% of people ask after finishing a good book. And do you know what happens when they ask that question... they look, and buy more of your books, if any are available. That author just flipped one gram into two. Well what if they have up words of five or ten books published? They just flipped that gram into an ounce. If they pump out 1 or 2 books a year on top of their five or ten, well they just flipped those ounces into bank baby!

It ain't no secret that some cats have made dump trucks full of cash off of one book. But the reality is that most folks who are successful 'working' authors have a catalog of books they've published. And that one book that really takes off is rarely they're first book. There's a FB group called "20 Books to $50k". The goal of each member in this little "club" is to pump out 20 decent books, which in turn should make them on average $50,000 a year. The reason they chose 20 books is because, in theory (which the majority of members have succeeded in), even if each book doesn't make a ton of money annually, the accumulation of 20 books will generate a large check every year.

    Geo and I are lifers, well condemned actually. I personally am happy with raking in $10-$20k a year. That's more money then I can spend in prison, and it allows me the opportunity to be generous with others around me, as well as with the people I love on the streets. It can also allow me to buy influence and favor in prison, thus making it a smoother ride for me. It is not an impossible, or even really a difficult task for someone in prison to make that much money a year, it just takes dedication to your craft. Think of the farmer who plants many seeds, she has a good harvest, if the farmer planted only one seed what kind of harvest would she have? Anyways, I'm getting long winded here, I'm gonna let Geo take over to explain more why this should be your business plan.

    Thanks Vinnie.
Look guys, it's easy to point to other authors and say I wish I could do that, or I bet they are making a fortune. I receive queries often that read like this: 'my pen is strong, my book will sell a million copies. Let's do a deal and split the money'.

    Of course they don't include any details about the book or a proper query. My response to these folks is a copy of: How to write a proper query. And, I mention that I've been doing this 14 years and all combined haven't sold a million copies, not even close.

    Had I stopped writing after doing Inmate Shopper I wouldn't be writing this book, I wouldn't be (as the internet states) one of the most published prisoners in America. It is called momentum, one book leads to another and another. The truth is, there are several people in prison who have sold more books and magazines than me, but I've had more books published than most. There's a difference. Sure, it's golden to write one book and have it do well, or really well but that is the exception. I've had many books that didn't sell or didn't break even, it's not a good feeling.

SELL YOUR BOOKS FROM PRISON

So don't look at me and think, George has the magic touch, or he's selling millions of copies, not true. My secret, I never gave up, I never rang the bell.

That doesn't mean there weren't days I wanted to, this shit is hard and frustrating and messes with your head, especially so as prisoners.

Fun Fact: 63% of Cadmus authors have written more than one book.

Back in 2009, before there were any formal resource books for prisoners, I offered Inmate Shopper to some 30 publishing companies, all said No thanks. But I believed in it, I knew there was a market for it because I knew there were more people like me in prison who needed the same resources I needed. So I scrapped together the money and helpers and published it myself in 2010, it is still the #1 selling prisoner resource in America. Now published by Freebird Publishers as I sold it and a few other of my titles in 2015 after a near fatal health issue. After six months of retirement, I was bored and started Prison Living Press, then sold in 2022.

Chapter 27

WRITING FROM PRISON and THE LAW.

Being proud to be a Convict: Leveraging your lock up, and the truth about "Son Of Sam Laws"

Geo and I have laid this science down to you many times already, but how about a ReUp for good measure? YOUR AN INTERESTING PERSON.... OUTLAWS ARE AS AMERICANA AS APPLE PIE.... SELL YOURSELF, BECAUSE YOUR NETWORK IS YOUR NET WORTH. Do not be ashamed of your past. Be remorseful, and treat it as the ultimate learning experience, at least publicly. But there's no reason you should be ashamed and hide it. Pen names are a worthy thing because it allows you to protect yourself from many things, like being brought to civil court by a victims family for restitution. Think of OJ Simpson. But your story can actually be a selling point, even if you use a pen name.

Charles Manson had hundreds of "fans" writing him weekly, and he was married to various groupies who knows how many times. He made over a million dollars during his incarceration just by selling his art work and sculptures. The same thing has happened with our local Arizona celebrity psychopath, Jodi Arias. These people, and others, have capitalized off of their criminality and infamy. Why shouldn't you?

Is it because you've been told that you can't make any money from selling books as a prisoner? Or maybe you've heard you can't profit off stories about your life or criminal history? What your taking about are called the Son Of Sam laws, enacted in New York during the late 1970's in order to prevent serial killer

SELL YOUR BOOKS FROM PRISON

David Berkowitz (the Son of Sam Killer) from making the millions of dollars being offered to him to tell his story by publishing companies. In 1991 the U.S Supreme Court ruled this law as unconstitutional in a case regarding the book "Wiseguy" by Nicholas Pileggi and Henry Hill (they even made it into a movie called Goodfellas, maybe you've seen it...).

As for convicts not having the right to write, well that was taken care by the legend himself, Mumia Abu Jamal. In the suit "Mumia Abu Jamal v. Price", the Supreme Court once again sided with the convict populace, basically saying that we cannot have our First Amendment rights stomped on, and that we are infact allowed to write, publish, and profit from any books we create.

In 2007 the Supreme court ONCE AGAIN had our backs (I know, ain't it crazy lol?), declaring that free speech was to be granted to the federal prison population, and that the Federal Bureau of Prisons personal "Son Of Sam" policy was unconstitutional.

So thanks a lot for all the support US Supreme court, even though you've denied a bunch of my friends appeals stating that they can be executed.... YOU ASSHOLES!

GEORGE R. KAYER AND VINNIE VALE

AFTER WORD:
How this book came about is a fluke, a rarity in publishing and a testimony to the bizarro karma circle of life. A few years ago Vinnie and I nearly came to blows and hadn't spoken to each other in years.

Then the guy moves in two doors down, OH Shit. Fortunately, Vinnie had rounded off some of his rough edges and chilled out since our last encounters. A few months ago he asked me a few questions about a book he is working on. Then he asked me to look at his book and tell him my thoughts. So I did.

I noticed his natural talent and some months later, after I bought Cadmus I ask Vinnie if he would write up a bunch of FAQs for us with his gregarious flair. Several times he ask: how do you want me to do this? Each time I said, be you, write just like you talk. You're funny and entertaining, have confidence in who you are. Once he saw my confidence in him he wrote those FAQs and nailed it. They're here in the back of the book.

After that, I knew the marketplace had a need for this book, written by prisoners for prisoners but since buying Cadmus my spare time is in short supply. I approached Vinnie once again and ask him if he would write this book with me. Again, he expressed a lack of confidence until I showed him a book he was familiar with, Write and Get Paid by Anthony Tisdale. I grabbed Anthony's book, opened it up to random page and said read me five lines. Vinnie did so. I ask, is that some boring shit or what? Vinnie concurred. (to be clear to the readers, I'm not clowning Tisdale's book rather the formal style of writing) I said there's 50 boring, How To Sell Books, out there, our book won't be boring!! It will be like the FAQs which are anything but boring. Vinnie said, I can do that!

Then Vinnie ask, how long do I have to write this?

I said, 30 days. He looked me dead in the eyes and saw I wasn't joking.

Okay, I'll get started tonight, he said.

As I write this it is our 28th day on the project. I've written a number of other books with people but never have I had so much fun as this project. Vinnie has been a delight to work with,

SELL YOUR BOOKS FROM PRISON

we often would laugh out loud when discussing vernacular and just how far to the edge to take the readers. Publishing has always been and still is a stuffed shirt , nose in the air business so we wanted to bring some humor and levity to it. To speak to our people in our language and let them know: Be your fucking self, that's all ya gotta do.

Geo out.

GLOSSARY OF TERMS

#10 Envelope- A standard, business sized envelope.

Agent- A liaison between a writer and editor or publisher. An agent shops a MS around, receiving a commission when the MS is accepted. Agents usually take 10-15% fee from advance and royalties.

ARC- Advanced Reader Copy.

Assignment- When an editor asks a writer to produce a specific article for an agreed upon fee.

Auction- Publishers sometimes bid for the acquisition of a book MS that has excellent sales potential. The bids are for the amount of the authors advance, advertising, and promotional expenses, royalty percentage, etc. Auctions are conducted by agents.

Backlist- A publishers list of books that were not published during the current season, but are still in print.

Beer Goggles- The term used to describe a state of being when one has consumed to much of a good thing, such as alcohol, or in an authors case, overwhelming joy. This disruptive state leaves the victims judgment impaired, so they will be unable to determine the attractiveness of a "situation", and therefore will most likely make very bad decisions with it. In the case of an author, it is when they read their manuscript immediately upon completion, because they will fail to see its "ugliness".

Beta Readers/Beta Testing- Beta Readers is the stage in pre-publishing when the manuscript is given to people to read, and give input and criticism. These readers are called Beta Readers/Testers. The slang term for Beta Testing is "Joy Riding".

Bimonthly- Every 2 months.

Bio- A sentence or brief paragraph about the writer can include education and work experience.

Blog- Short for weblog. Used by writers to build a platform by posting regular commentary, observations, poems, tips, etc.

Blurb- The copy on paperback book covers or hard cover book dust jackets, either promoting the book and the author or featuring testimonials from book reviewers or well-known people in the books field. Also called flap copy or jacket copy.

Boilerplate- A standardized contract.

Byline- Name of the author appearing with the published piece.

Chapbook- A small usually paperback booklet of poetry, ballads, or tales.

Circulation- The number of subscribers to a magazine.

Clips- Samples, usually from newspapers or magazines, of a writers published work.

Coffee-Table Book- A heavily illustrated oversize book.

Commercial Novels- Novels designed to appeal to a broad audience. These are often broken down into categories such as western, mystery, and romance. (SEE "GENRE")

Contributors Copies- Copies of the issues of magazines sent to the author in which the writers work appears.

Co-Publishing- Arrangement where author and publisher share publication costs and profits of a book. Also known as co-operative publishing.

Copyediting- Editing a MS for grammar, punctuation, printing style, and factual accuracy.

Copyright- A means to protect an authors work. See Registered copyright.

Cover Letter- A brief letter that accompanies the MS being sent to an agent, editor or publisher.

Creative Nonfiction- Nonfictional writing that uses an innovative approach to the subject and creative language.

Critiquing Service- An editing service in which writers pay a fee for comments on the salability or other qualities of their MS.

CV- Curriculum Vita. A brief listing of qualifications and career accomplishments.

Editing- is the removing of mistakes in a manuscript before publication, also the process of making the story more interesting than the first or second draft.

Electronic Rights- Secondary or subsidiary rights dealing with electronic/multimedia formats (I.e., the internet, electronic magazines).

Erotica- Fiction that is sexually oriented.

Evaluation Fees- Fees an agent may charge to evaluate material. The extent and quality of this evaluation varies, but comments usually concern salability of the MS.

Fair Use- A provision of the copyright law that says short passages from copyrighted material may be used without infringing on the owners rights.

Feature- An article giving the reader information of human interest rather than news.

Filler- A short item used by an editor to "fill" out a newspaper column or magazine page. It could be a joke, an anecdote, etc.

SELL YOUR BOOKS FROM PRISON

Film Rights- Rights sold or optioned by the agent/author to a person in the film industry, enabling the book to be made into a movie.

Foreign Rights- Translation or reprint rights to be sold abroad.

Frontlist- A publishers lost of books that are new to the current season.

Game- The slang term used to describe a hustle or system of ingrained practices such as the publishing industry. Also used to describe a thing or process that is difficult to learn, which is taught by someone who has skill and knowledge in the subject.

Genre- Refers either to a general classification of writing, such as the novel or the poem, or to the categories within those classifications, such as the problem novel or the sonnet.

Ghostwriter- Writer who puts into literary form an article, speech, story, or book based on another persons ideas or knowledge.

Graphic Novel- A story in graphic form, long comic strip, or heavily illustrated story of 40 pages or more in book format.

Hi-Lo- A type of fiction that offers a high level of interest for readers at a low reading level.

High Concept- A story idea easily expressed in a quick, one line description.

Hook- Aspect of the work that sets it apart from others and draws in the reader/viewer.

How To- Books and magazine articles offering a combination of information and advice in describing how something can be accomplished.

Imprint- Name applied to a publisher's specific line of books.

Like Prison Living Press is for Cadmus

    Joint Contract- A legal agreement between a publisher and two or more authors, establishing provisions for the division of royalties the book generates.

    Layout- Simply put, it is the design of the interior pages of a book. It includes: font type, font size, chapter headers, page headers and paragraph set up.

    Lead Time- The time between the acquisition of a MS by an editor and its actual publication.

    Literary Fiction- The general category of serious, non-formulaic, intelligent fiction

    Mainstream Fiction- Fiction that transcends popular novel categories such as mystery, romance, and science fiction.

    MS/MSS-Manuscript

    Marketing Fee- Fee charged by some agents to cover marketing expenses. It may be used to cover postage, telephone calls, faxes, photocopying, or any other expense incurred in marketing a MS.

    Mass Market- Nonspecialized books of wide appeal directed toward a large audience. Memoir- A narrative recounting a writers (or narrators) personal or family history specifics may be altered, though essentially considered nonfiction.

    Middle Grade or MG- The general classification of books written for readers approximately ages 9 to 11. Also called Middle Readers.

    Midlist- Those titles on a publishers list that are not expected to be big sellers, but are expected to have limited/modest sales.

    Multiple Contract- Book contract with an agreement for a

future book(s).

   Multiple Submissions- Sending more than one book or article idea to a publisher at the same time.

   Narrative Fiction- A narrative presentation of actual events.

   Net Royalty- A royalty payment based on the amount of money a book publisher receives on the sale of a book after booksellers discount, special discounts, and returns.

   Network- The accumulated lore and reputation that surrounds a person, as well as their web of contacts whether they be family, friends, or business.

   Novella- A short novel, or a long short story approximately 7,000 to 35,000 words.

   One-Time Rights- Rights allowing a MS to be published one time. The work can be sold again by the writer without violating the contract.

   Option Clause- A contract clause giving a publisher the right to publish an authors next book.

   Pen Name- The use of a name other than your legal name on articles, stories or books. Also called a pseudonym.
   PenPimping- The art of using your pen and writing skills to hustle something to others for the purpose of acquiring financial compensation, or some other form of gain. This can be used in the art of PenPal writing by selling yourself in order to ingratiate yourself with sympathetic strangers so they will give you money. In convict publishing it is the art of pimping out your writings/books to potential buyers, influencers, editors, or marketplaces.

   Picture book- a type of book aimed at preschoolers to 8yr olds that tells a story using a combination of text and artwork, or artwork only.

Platform- A writers speaking experience, interview skills, website, and other abilities which help form a following of potential buyers for that authors book.

Player- A "Vinnieism" that he uses no less than 100 times a day in conversation. To him it means more of "a participant in the game of life", and less as someone who participates in the life long jubilee of having multiple lovers.

POD- Print On Demand

Proofreading- Close reading and correction of a MS typographical errors.

Proposal- A summary of a proposed book submitted to a publisher, particularly used for nonfiction MS. A proposal often contains an individualized cover letter, one-page overview of the book, marketing information, competitive books, marketing information, chapter by chapter outline, and two to three sample chapters.

Query- A letter that sells an idea to an editor or agent. Usually a query is brief (no more than one page) and uses attention getting prose.

Reporting Time- The time it takes an editor to report to the author on his/her query or MS.

Royalties- A percentage of sales that an author can receive as negotiated in a contract. For instance, an author may receive 10% on the retail price of each book sold. These terms are negotiated in the book publishing contract and may be tied to any advance money and various payment periods throughout the year.

S.A.S.E- Self Addressed Stamped Envelope. Should be included with all correspondence.

Science- A slang term used to describe something that is difficult and complex. Also, to "be given the science" of something means to be educated in such by a person well versed in said topic. (SEE "GAME")

Self Publishing- In this arrangement the author pays for manufacturing, production and marketing of their book and keeps all income derived from the book sales.

Semimonthly- Twice per year.

Semiweekly- Twice per week.

Short Story- A complete short story of 1,500 words or fewer. Simultaneous Submissions- Sending the same article, story, or poem to several publishers at the same time. Some publishers refuse to consider such submissions.

Slant- The approach or style of a story or article that will appeal to readers of a specific magazine.

Slush pile- The stack of unsolicited or misdirected MS received by an editor or book publisher.

Social Networks- Websites that connect users: sometimes generally, other times around specific interests. For instance Facebook, X (formerly known as Twitter), Instagram, LinkedIn, Tiktok, etc.

Subsidiary Rights- All rights other than book publishing rights included in a book publishing contract, such as paperback rights, book club rights, and movie rights. Part of an agents job is to negotiate those rights and advise you on which to sell and which to keep. Synopsis- A brief summary of a story, novel or play. As part of a book proposal, it is a comprehensive summary condensed in a page or page and a half, single spaced.

Tearsheet- Page from a magazine or newspaper containing your printed story, article, poem, or ad.

Trade Book- Either a hardcover or softcover book subject matter frequently concerns a special interest for a general audience sold mainly in bookstores.

Trade Paperback- A soft bound volume published and designed for the general public available in many bookstores.

Trademark- Trademark: A legally protected symbol, name, or logo that distinguishes and identifies goods or services, representing a brand's unique identity and preventing confusion in the marketplace.

Translation Rights- Sold to a foreign agent or foreign publisher.

Trending- When something is Trending it implies that it has garnered a large amount of popularity that in turn inspires a legion of copycats, or followers. Usually reserved for something that gained popularity on the internet, but has become more integrated in the worlds lexicon to describe anything, no matter its source, that has become popular.

Vanity Publishing- This is similar to self publishing, but it often costs and can be done by predatory companies taking advantage of writers who are unfamiliar with publishing.

Whole Book Marketing- The concept that a book and its author as a whole are a marketing plan, not just the publicity aspect of publishing. For the author this encompasses everything from their name/pen name used, their appearance and persona, as well as their business acumen, and reputation as a person. For the book this encompasses everything as well, from the font, typeset, and layout of the words in the book, to the cover image, title etc. Finally the process of the publicity campaign once the book is finally released caps of the concept of Whole Book Marketing

YA- Young Adult books.

End of Glossary

SELL YOUR BOOKS FROM PRISON

SERVICES OFFERED BY CADMUS

Cadmus Publishing LLC.

CadmusPublishing.com | Fast-book-album-covers.com

BooksByPrisoners.com

info@cadmuspublishing.com | Facebook.com/CadmusPublishing

PO Box 8664, Haledon, NJ, 07538

Offering:

- Publishing
- Publishing services
- Marketing for music, magazines, books and newsletters.

Professional Associations

Independent Book Publishers of America.

Better Business Bureau - Accredited.

Chamber of Commerce, Haledon NJ.

GEORGE R. KAYER AND VINNIE VALE

EDITING AND TYPING

EDITING

We have three options: Full professional editing, AI (Artificial Intelligence) editing, faxes to your already digital MS. Professional editing: 1.2¢ per word.

AI: $40/hr. The computer editing software will run through the book almost instantly - the hourly rate is required for our editor to go through and approve (or not) each change it suggests.

Corrections on MS you send: If you send in a digital manuscript (not typed by us), be sure it is already corrected. We will have to charge per hour for corrections you make to a digital MS you had typed into the computer from outside.

Prison Tablets

Cadmus is one of the few Publishers who accept manuscripts and communicate using tablets. And, all of our materials are designed for our low resolution sucky tablets.

BONUS EXPOSURE FOR YOUR BOOK:

All new Cadmus authors are placed in our Interactive Bookstore. This bookstore is especially designed for people in prison and has many features so be sure to read our Marketing flyer for all the details.

Typing Service:

You probably don't have a computer - but modern publishers (including us) need a digital file. All package prices also assume we are receiving a digital file. Fortunately, we have typists on staff. Almost all of our incarcerated authors need this service, so we do provide a 25% discount. Includes on-the-fly editing! Need something besides a book typed? We type anything you need, including legal work!

Put simply: we do everything we can to help, from the final steps before publishing (like editing, beta readers, etc) to making your book stand out from all others with effective marketing and publicity... we are at your side.

We have assembled the best staff. We outsource nothing overseas, ever, and handle all communication personally. You will have a direct line to your Author Liaison, who is there to ensure your book is done the way you envisioned it. One of our owners is George Kayer, one of the most published prisoners in America. Our other owner is Ken, an x-offender. They know the difficulties you live with.

We work with you. Sadly, too few publishers are willing to work with the incarcerated. Torturously, we understand how the system works and are here to work with you.

Shop Around-Please then, you'll see for yourself that our prices are competitive or lower than others. We do. Our personal if they communicate on tablets? We do. Our personal customer service is why our authors return.

LOWEST TYPING FEES! If you need your work put into the computer (unless you have someone else typing for you on the outside, this is probably true), this can be a huge savings for you. This service and discount is available even if you do not publish with us, and just need the typing.

We accept prison phone calls. We know the drill. (They must be pre-paid, though, not collect).

$50 Referrals! If you have a book with us (either in-progress or already published) and you refer a friend who publishes, print both with us, you will receive a $50 referral fee sent to your people or put directly to your account at your destination.

Royalties: The simple answer is: we try to make sure you earn a minimum of 20% of the cover price of your book. Once your book is completed and uploaded for distribution we can provide exact numbers. For more on royalties ask for...

We would like to thank you for considering Cadmus Publishing to work with you on *making your book a reality.* We know that uncounted weeks, months, possibly even years have gone into writing your book to be the best it can be; and, it deserves nothing but the best. We can provide you with the best available services for your project, at the best available price for your budget.

Settle in for a ton of info.

We have tried to get as much in here as possible, on just one sheet so that it abides by as many institution rules as possible, but we do a lot of stuff. So this is densely packed with info, and not a lot of pretty design we generally take so much pride in. So bear with us! If you still have questions, just ask your Author Liaison. He/she will be happy to answer them!

We'd like to take this opportunity to introduce you to who we are, what we do, and why you - and your book - need us.

To begin with, all of our publishing packages carry everything you need to get your book *printed, published, and available worldwide to all major retailers,* and available worldwide to all major smaller retailers as well, in addition to libraries or whoever else carries books. That's right - your book will be available around the world. In addition - *You retain all rights and copyrights.*

Cadmus Publishing LLC
PO Box 8664
Haledon, NJ 07538
360-565-6459 (Mon-Fri 9AM-5PM, Eastern Time)
email: info@CadmusPublishing.com
web: www.CadmusPublishing.com

SELL YOUR BOOKS FROM PRISON

CHOOSE PACKAGES OR INDIVIDUAL SERVICES
(✓ charts ALL of our Package options, which everything you can get as an individual service, things (or upgrades) for any package.)

ENJOY OUR LOW PRICES	eBook $449	Standard $299 $699	ProStyle $1299 $1195	Silver $1699 $1699	Gold $2699 $2050	Platinum $3799 $5999	Ultimate $4299 $11474
E-Pub	✓	✓	✓	✓	✓	✓	✓
Paperback		✓	✓	✓	✓	✓	✓
Hardcover				✓	✓	✓	✓
Standard Formatting	✓	✓	✓	✓	✓	✓	✓
Free ISBN		✓	✓	✓	✓	✓	✓
Amazon Look Inside	✓	✓	✓	✓	✓	✓	✓
B&N Read Instantly	✓	✓	✓	✓	✓	✓	✓
Books in Print Database	✗	✓	✓	✓	✓	✓	✓
Bookstore Returnability	✗	Optional	Optional	Optional	Optional	Optional	✓
Cover Type	Tier 1	Tier 1	Tier 2	Tier 2+	Any	Any	Any
Author Webpage	✗	Standard	1 Yr Slvr	3 Yr Slvr	3 Yr Plat	3 Yr Plat	3 Yr Plat
Image Copies (PB/HC)	✗	1/0	2/0	5/1	10/2	25/5	50/10
Image Insertions	✗	10	25	75	100	200	No Limit
LCCN					✓	✓	✓
Copyright Registration			25,000	50,000	100,000	175,000	250,000
Typing*			Tier 2	Write-Up	Basic	Basic	Advanced
Press Release				1@2 mos	2@3 mos	3@3 mos	3@6 mos
Internet Ads**				Tier 1	Tier 2	Tier 3	Tier 4
Social Media				Starter	Starter	Pro	Pro
Marketing Kit		✓	✓	5	10	20	30
Reader Reviews		✓	✓	5	10	20	50
Book Blogger Submission			✓	✓	35,000	75,000	150,000
100% Royalties	✓	✓	✓	✓	✓	✓	✓
Copyediting***						Choose 1	All 3
Professional Reviews							
AudioBook						25% Off	40% Off

* Lists how many words of free typing (based on typed original, for handwritten original, included word count is half of what is shown). Standard typing rates: $1.79 per 250 words from typed original (MS typed with ribbon may cost more); $2.81 per 250 words from handwritten original. You can use prison email or send your M/S to us at a rate of $1 per 1,000 words. Mailing a complete MS from non-prison email carries no charges. Please ensure the spelling and punctuation etc. is to your satisfaction we will not look over unless you have us edit it.

** Denotes how many sites, then for how many months. For example, "2@3 mos" means you pick two sites (options are Google, Facebook, Amazon) and they will run for 3 months.

*** Lists how many words of free copyediting.

Didn't publish with us, but wish you had? Talk to us about bringing your project over to our platform from your current publisher - and reap all the benefits, services, and more that we provide!

Want to publish with us, but don't have all the funds needed? Set up your account with us and the funds as you get them, and we can start once you're at ~5%.

Didn't publish with us, but still want to use some of our services? No a problem! We can work with your book from another publisher for many of our services!

Copyright Registration Add-On: $175. Includes all government fees. And mailing a copy of your book (with their address label) to the Office of Copyrights and Trademarks. This is the ultimate protection from theft of your work.

Library of Congress Control Number Add-On: $79. This is the number that shows to the government that your book exists and the number that any library, and some retailers use to order it. This is different from your ISBN or copyright, and cannot be done after the book is published.

Book Covers and AI Covers:
You can always provide your own, completed cover art work for us to scan in and use. You've heard about AI art, we now have a fleet new AI designer for affordable AI book covers. Ask for more info.

Tier 1: $50. We find a stock image/art online that matches your idea as close as possible. There's no image manipulation, so what we can find is what gets put on.

Tier 2: $100. We find up to five stock images and use photoshop to put them together as well as possible.

Tier 2+: means Tier 2, or you can get 50% off a custom cover.

Custom: Whatever you want, costs can vary; but expect to start at $150.

What is...

Books In Print Database: Every one of our print packages includes the Books In Print database inclusion automatically. This database is used by libraries worldwide to find titles, create lists, and decide which titles to offer.

"Look Inside" & "Read Instantly": In a physical bookstore, you can flip pages to get a taste of the book before you buy it. These features are how readers preview your book online.

Additional Formats!

Translations: 1¾¢ per word. We can translate your book into most major languages, including Spanish, German, Russian, French, Romanian, and more.

AudioBook conversion: 2¢ per word, + $75 setup fee. Professional voice actor, professional studio.

Done with this flyer? Feel free to leave of our for someone else to use!

GEORGE R. KAYER AND VINNIE VALE

Fast-Book-Album-Covers.com
FAST AND AFFORDABLE
BOOK AND ALBUM COVERS

DON'T WAIT months for your cover designs!

We do beautiful, eye catching, professional covers in a week or less.

PRICES STARTING AT $50 — Use Code 3OFFCOVERS for a 30% discount on your next cover order

Music By Prisoners: Starter Package

Music By Prisoners: Starter Package	Price
Basic Vocal Additons & Effects	
Vocal Clean-Up	$300
Basic Mixing & Mastering	
Pick Your Own Beat From the Library / Use Your Own Beat	

PO BOX 8664 Haledon, NJ 07538
info@CadmusPublishing.com
Ph: 360-565-6459
www.CadmusPublishing.com

SELL YOUR BOOKS FROM PRISON

Music By Prisoners Services

	Song Duration		
	Up to 2 minutes	2 to 3 minutes	3+ minutes
Production			
Vocals Processing			
Quantization (If your performance gets out of rythm with the beat tempo too much, this will be necessary)	$80.00	$100.00	
Vocals Clean-Up / Enhancement	$100.00		
Vocals Add-Ons			
Harmonies (Record vocal harmonies on our side for specific sections)	$40.00	$60.00	$80.00
Backing Vocals (Record backing vocals on our side to emphasize sections)	$40.00	$60.00	$40.00
Instrumentation / Composition			
Basic (drums/bass/+1 instrument)	$200.00	$220.00	$240.00
Advanced (Basic + multiple instruments layering)	$240.00	$260.00	$290.00
Pro (Advanced + Complex instrumentation, harmonies & rytmic variations)	$300.00	$340.00	$360.00
If you want specific real instruments (like a sax solo section), we may have to hire a musician depending on the instrument	$50 to $150 (depends on different factors)		
Mixing			
Basic up to 10 tracks	$150.00	$170.00	$190.00
Basic 10+ tracks	$180.00	$200.00	$220.00
Pro up to 10 tracks	$240.00	$270.00	$300.00
Pro 10+ tracks	$280.00	$330.00	$360.00
Mastering			
Basic	$100.00		
Pro	$150.00		
Distribution (per song, yearly suscription)			
EVERY music streaming platform (Spotify, Itunes, YouTube Music, Tidal, etc) - 150+ platforms	$40 / yearly		
Make it available on social medias (Instagram, Facebook, TikTok, CapCut, etc)	$10 / yearly		
Marketing			
AI Cover Art	$60.00		
Composite Cover Art	$100.00		
Spotify, Apple Music & YouTube Artist Profile (Profile picture, Banner, Artist Bio)	$120.00		
Artist Verification (Blue checkmark on Spotify & YouTube artist profile)	$40.00		
Spotify Editorial Playlists Pitching	$25.00		
Others			
Music By Prisoners Website	Set up & 1st year: $40 - Renewal: $20		
Banking service for your royalties (No charge for Cadmus Authors)	Account set up: $25 - $8 per quarter - Royalties paid quarterly		
15 min Consultation with producer (phone call or recorded)	1st is free - $20 per follow-up		
Song Revisions (If you want to make specific changes to the song)	1st is free - $75 to $150 per extra revision (depending on the amount of work)		

GEORGE R. KAYER AND VINNIE VALE

Music by Prisoners: Starter Package F.A.Q.

- What is the "Starter Package" and what does it include?
Our "Starter" service is our most basic music service. Here you will have to pick a beat from our library or use your own. The beats on our library are not exclusive and won't be able to have ownership by you because they are not made/produced by Cadmus, meaning it won't be able to be distributed or sold. This service is perfect if you just want to make a song for a loved one or for yourself. We would just need to record your vocals on top of the beat and mix them to have a full track. We won't be able to modify the beat nor change the sound of it.
It includes vocals clean-up and enhancement plus basic mixing and mastering.

- Can I distribute/sell my Starter Package song?
The only situation where you will be able to distribute and sell your starter package song, is if you have your own beat and own the full rights to it. Unfortunately, if you nor Cadmus have the full rights of the beat, it won't be allowed to be distributed or sold because of copyright issues.
In the case your song is able to be distributed, we offer distribution options which you can find on our MBP services price sheet.

- How does the process go?
This is a simpler process:
1) Pick your beat.
2) Record your vocals on top of the beat.
3) Producer does the necessary basic edits to your vocals plus a basic mixing and mastering to the track.
4) Your song is ready!

- What beat can I use?
You can use your own beat or pick one from Cadmus pre-made beats library. Keep in mind that the beats in the library are non exclusive and are not made by our producer.

SELL YOUR BOOKS FROM PRISON

Music By Prisoners: F.A.Q.

- Do you have a producer?
Yes, our producer is a Berklee College of Music graduate trained in the highest standards of the music industry. He has 10+ years of experience and has worked with multiple artists in various styles.

- What styles/genres can be produced?
We can work with any kind of genre.

- How does the process go and how long does it take from start to finish?
This is the ideal process.
1) Making the beat. If you already have one, then we either skip this part, or add/modify stuff if you want. If we make it from scratch, then we need to make sure everyone is happy with it before moving to the next step. This might mean going back and forth between you and the producer until we reach the perfect beat for you.
2) Record your vocals. The reason this goes after having the beat ready is because you need to be listening to the beat with headphones in order for you to be able to record your vocals on time and match the beat.
3) Mixing. Now that we have your vocals recorded, it's time to mix them with the beat and see if we have any recording issues. If we do (which hopefully won't happen) we may have to record your vocals again. If not, we move to mixing.
4) Mastering. Having the mix ready, we can master your song and make it sound big and loud.
5) Review. Now that everything is done, the song will be sent for you to review. If you are not happy with some parts or aspects, then we go back to editing the beat and repeat the necessary processes.
6) Distribution. The song is ready, everyone is happy. Time to send it to the music platforms and make your song go LIVE!
The amount of time this process will take will ultimately depend on many factors, such as communication efficiency/speed. If we need to re-record vocals, how many revisions, etc. It can range from 7 to 20+ days depending on those factors.

- Can I use a beat I already have?
Yes. The only requirement here is that the beat is copyright free or that you own the full rights to it. We cannot distribute it if the beat doesn't meet those requirements.

- Can we create a beat from scratch?
Yes. Moreover, this is recommended. By doing this, not only can we make sure that you will own all the rights to the music, it also means we can make a fully personalized beat for you and do our best to make the music in your head a reality.

- What if I don't have all my lyrics finished? Can I get help with that?
Absolutely, we also offer a service of lyric writing if you need any help with that. It can be a whole section or maybe just a few sentences. Whatever you need.

- How should I record my vocals?
The ideal situation would be having you record your vocals into a digital recorder. By doing this, we can get the best quality recording possible in a non-studio situation. It is very important to make sure there are as little (ideally none) background sounds/voices at the time of recording your voice.
If you can't, we will have to record your vocals through a phone call. This will require extra production steps in order to "restore" and "enhance" the quality of the recording as much as possible. We will do our best to enhance your vocals in these situations, although the final results will never be as good as with the digital recorder.

- What does 'numbers of tracks' mean in the price sheet?
The tracks inside a music project are the different layers that make up the song as a whole. For example, one track would be your vocals, another would be the bass, another an instrument (a synth for example) and so on. The number of layers will ultimately depend on the complexity of the song. Some songs can even go up to 60+ tracks, and a lot more!

GEORGE R. KAYER AND VINNIE VALE

- Is mixing and mastering necessary?

Mixing and mastering is the sound engineering part of the song development. When the song is fully produced with the vocals ready and everything in position, we move to the mixing side. After mixing, we do the mastering, which is a process done to the song as a whole.

In order to meet the industry standards, it is necessary to have at least a basic mixing/mastering on the song. We do recommend going pro with this, since it will give your song much better quality and will ensure the best possible listening experience.

- What is mixing?

Mixing is the process of combining all the individual tracks or elements of a song into a final, cohesive piece of music. Imagine you have separate recordings for vocals, guitars, drums, and other instruments. Mixing is like putting together a puzzle, making sure each piece fits well and sounds good together. It involves carefully applying EQs, pannings, compressions, exciters, saturations, reverbs, effects, etc. to each individual track in the song.

- What is mastering?

Mastering is the final step in music production, refining a song for optimal sound quality. It involves technical adjustments, ensuring balanced frequencies and consistent volume by taking the mixed song and preparing it for various playback systems (like headphones, car speakers, or club sound systems) to ensure it sounds great everywhere.

Crucial for wide distribution, it corrects imperfections and adheres to industry standards, enhancing the overall impact of the music.

- Where is my music going to be available?

We will distribute your music to every existing music streaming platform. This will obviously include the most popular like Spotify, iTunes, Amazon Music, YouTube, Tidal, etc. It will go live on a total of 150+ streaming platforms.

- How will I make money from my music?

You will earn royalties per song stream. The cumulation of every stream on every platform will then be received as streaming and publishing revenue. We can also sell your music online by charging per download.

3

- What does "artist verification" on the artist profile mean?

Have you seen or heard about the "blue checkmark" some people have on their social media? This is kind of the same thing, but in your Spotify artist profile. It means you are now verified as an authentic artist, giving you more credibility and exposure.

- What is the Spotify editorial playlist pitching?

It is recommended to leave a 3 week space from the time we sent your song to be distributed to the day it goes live. This is with the purpose of letting the streaming platforms review your song and get the chance to be featured in their editorial playlists. Getting into those playlists means a HUGE amount of exposure. After the first day your song gets sent, you can send a pitch to the editorial teams with the hopes of getting better chances to be featured on one of their playlists.

This cannot be guaranteed, since it will ultimately depend on their side. The chances are small but get higher as you release more music and promote it efficiently.

- What if I don't have access to a digital recorder?

We can schedule a phone call to record your voice through the call. It will be very important for you to make sure there are no audible background sounds/voices (at least the minimum possible). The more isolated your voice can be, the better job we can do at enhancing the recording in post production.

- How do I collect my royalties?

1) If you publish as an independent you may direct your royalties to any bank account you choose.

2) If you do not have a bank account and use our Music by Prisoners label your royalties will be deposited to our account and paid by us quarterly (every three months).

PO BOX 8664 Haledon, NJ 07538
info@CadmusPublishing.com
Ph: 360-565-6859
www.CadmusPublishing.com

4

SELL YOUR BOOKS FROM PRISON

FREQUENTLY ASKED QUESTIONS (FAQS)

There's much more to publishing a book from prison than writing and printing it: typing the handwritten manuscript in a digital file, then the mechanical editing of said manuscript by an editor to correct grammar, punctuation, spelling, and inconsistencies; proofreading galleys and page proofs; providing "print-ready" charts, maps, graphs, photographs, or illustrations, if included; organizing page layout, and deciding what on which pages; designing the front and back cover; then there's formatting the nearly complete digital file into the formats specific to eBook and Print On Demand. And that's not even the half of it, after all that you then have to secure a copyright, an ISBN, an LCCN, and apply barcodes. THEN were ready for the book release and marketing, and that's when the overwhelming part begins. Think you can accomplish all that from your prison unit? Allow me to save you the headache of attempting and inform you that the answer is as close to "no" as you can get. Unless your a real specific type of individual, your gonna need Cadmus Publishing.

I've put together an F.A.Q to answer the questions I most often get asked, as well as cover any potential questions you may have as you progress in your schooling of the publishing industry. Most of you are fish to this publishing game, so please allow us to be your proverbial "Big Homie", and run down the convict code of publishing to you.

Q: If 1 million people self-publish their own books every year from their living rooms, why do I need to pay you to do it for me?

A: The short answer is, because their at home in their living rooms with a computer, and your sitting in a prison cell dealing with tyrannical officers and uncountable "security" restrictions. The common misconception with self-publishing is that its a simple 3 step processes,
1) write a book
2) upload it to Amazon
3) cash royalty checks
Unfortunately, its not that simple, in fact its quite difficult and

costly.

Many people on the street become frustrated when they're asked how they want their book formatted, what kind of ISBN, or Lccn. Then there's a correct book size for each genre, font styles, distribution choices: eBook, paperback, hardcover and each require their own ISBN's. What about editing? There's copy editing, content editing, image editing for graphics, charts, diagrams and photos.

Even if you have a strong dedicated network of people such as family members on the streets to assist you, unless they have publishing experience the task of self-publishing from prison is nearly impossible without professional help. It almost feels impossible even if YOU DO have an extended network. In debating whether or not to self-publish entirely by yourself, or publish through our publishing house, consider this. Is your manuscript hand written? Well go try and figure out how to get that typed up into a digital copy, then come talk to me. And that's not even step 1.

Q: Why should I choose Cadmus Publishing over any of the other houses out there? I'm sure I can find one that's cheaper.

A: We invite everyone to shop around. Get our brochure and you'll see we offer every service needed for pre-publishing, publishing and post publishing marketing. We have the largest distribution network from Walmart to Warsaw Poland, the EU and South America, and of course Amazon.

We also come with a large staff of experienced O.Gs in the publishing game, and our name will be on your book just as much as yours will be. Why would we want to put out crap? Anyone who's had to slang street pharmaceuticals knows that if you step on your product to much, your gonna lose your clientele to the pharmacist down the block. You may have been the king of copper stripping on the street and think: I got this publishing thing down, I don't need no guys in suits trying to get in my pocket! Okay bro, when this little publishing thing kicks your ass, we'll be here with the Band-Aids and a shot of tequila.

Q: Well, if there are other publishing houses, what difference does it make which publisher I use?

A: You have to understand the difference's between publishing houses. You have 3 main structures of publishers, a vanity press, a publishing services company, and a real full service publishing house. A vanity press basically takes your MS, and with the whackest effort necessary, they cobble your book together and kick you out the door. Its your job to do all the rest. They have poor relations with their customers, because that's all you are to them, a customer.

A publishing services company like Freebird or Lockdown Publications are a step up from vanity printers. They provide placement or distributors like Amazon, collect and distribute royalties but offer few marketing options. They have better relationships with their customers, but once again, your still just a customer.

A real, full service publishing house is what people think of when it comes to publishing, like Random House, Hurst, or Little Brown and Co. Cadmus is in this category. They offer literally everything publishing and marketing service, social, bloggers, book reviews, Google ads and much much more. They also accept queries for regular publishing just like Random House, Hurst, or Little Brown.

Q: What's all this talk of ISBN, and LCCN. These sound like four letter words to me, why should I care about them?

A: ISBN stands for "International Standard Book Number", and if you don't know the ins and outs of handling an ISBN it can cause one to have IBS, Irritable Bowel Syndrome. An ISBN identifies the registration(publisher), title, edition, and format. It is assigned to each separate edition and variation (except reprintings) of a publication. For example, an eBook, a paperback, and a hardcover edition of the same book will each have their own ISBN. It is a unique and unchangeable number identifying one title by one publisher. An example of a Cadmus ISBN is 978-1-63751-362-0 which identifies " The Inmates Guide To Success As An Author" by Francis Raemond (which I highly recommend you pick up). The 978- is the general prefix element assigned to all ISBN's the 1-6 denotes the registration group such as language, county group, etc. the 3751- denotes the registrant, or publisher the 362- denotes the publication element, or the specific book and format and the 0 is the "check digit".

LCCN stands for Library of Congress Control Number and is the serial based system of numbering cataloged records in the Library of Congress. In its most basic form, the number includes a year and a serial number. The year has 4 digits, and the serial number has 6 digits and should include leading 0's

Q: What does M.S mean, I knew a guy on the yard named Chino that rapped the MS. Is he an author?

A: M.S stands for "manuscript", and has nothing to do with any kind of local Hispanic unions. A manuscript is traditionally any document written by an author by hand or typewriter, prior to being published. If you've got a hand written book sitting in your cell, that is a MS homeboy

Q: What the hell is a barcode, is that some kind of slang term for the convict code?

A: Well a guy walks into a bar and asks the bartender to make him a barcode, and the bartender says "how do I make a barcode?" and the guy says "how the hell should I know, your the bartender". If you have to ask, then you need us to do it for ya. We at Cadmus can legally produce our own barcodes, so we got you player. To sum it up in the simplest terms home, its the thing that makes the cash register beep and check out when they scan it at the check out. Every book has to have one.

Q: Why do I need you to edit my book, can't I just do it with a dictionary?

A: Oh that would be hilarious. But unfortunately, there's a lot more that goes into editing than spelling. Ask yourself this, do you know the difference between copy editing, continuity/style editing, or content editing? Basically right now your MS is most likely in what's called a "draft stage". What we do is hone the language, and get them word shanks sharp for the yard then we rectify grammatical errors and put them on a solid 2 a day program till their on hub status. After all is said and done, your MS will leave the gates a yoked up slung down book, with its chin up and chest out. (On a side note, we do offer all forms of editing.)

Q: So tell me the truth, does the small print in the contract says I'm signing the rights of my book(s) over to you?

A: That's a big negative ghost rider. You own what you create. We just assist you in making your vision a reality. You own and retain 100% of all legal Rights to you book. Sell it to Hollywood player..

Q: Well that sounds cool, but what exactly am I going to have to pay in order to see my vision into a reality?

A: Rough estimate is between $, and $$$. It all comes down to exactly what you want or need. Our packaging system was designed to offer our wide range of services in various formats. Everything from basic publishing, all the way up to advanced publishing with marketing and social media support.

Q: Can my book(s) be converted into EBooks? I heard you aren't a real author unless your book can be read on an IPad by fancy people.

A: Yea absolutely. All of our publishing packages include an EBook for online reading or downloadable to use on any of the common devices capable of e-reading owned by almost everyone on earth, fancy or not.

Q: What does the 2000s era rap-metal band P.O.D have to do with the publishing industry?

A: What the hell are you talking about? They have absolutely nothing to do with it (that I know of). P.O.D refers to Print-On-Demand, which means only one book is printed at a time. Your book(s) is held in a file storage system by the book printing company, until someone in the Southtown or wherever else orders a paperback copy, at which time the book(s) will be printed and shipped. This is why ALL book files must be in digital format.

Q: How long will it take for you to complete my book? Are we talking like a week, or month? I got bills to pay player.

A: You should probably lay off the 2 for 1s dogg. Short answer, no clue. Each project is different and requires its own timeline. I'm not even gonna try and predict an end date. You want prophecy, call Madame Cleo. Here are some variables that affect how long it takes to get your title published. If we have to mail your manuscript to you for final authorization? How long will the mailroom hold it before delivery? How many pages, how many changes you make. How many customers are ahead of you, how many add on services you order.

Q: I'm a cold ass player because I already got my book published and distributed through some other cats, I just can't seem to sell any copies. Can you hook a player up with some of them marketing services?

A: Ooo baby you bad, congrats for getting that book cooked up on your own! The answer is absolutely yes! Hit me up homeboy or girl, I got you. We offer a wide range of marketing services : Amazon marketing services, Google ads, bloggers, book reviewers, websites, social media support, posters, bookmarks, t-shirts with your book cover and more. No other publishing services company has more options for selling your book than Cadmus.

Q: Will you read my story for free and tell me how amazing it is and how rich it will make me?

A: ....No. Not because I'm being a turd, but anyone who wants to charge you a reading fee to EVALUATE the salability of your book is gaming you. No one can predict which book, movie, song or TV show will make fat stacks.

SELL YOUR BOOKS FROM PRISON

Meta ads.

This is much more involved than tossing an ad on Meta and hope it does well. Any business or friend that does that for you is flushing your money down the toilet. Here's what we do for for our ads and our clients. Short version.

Step 1. Identify the most searched keywords for your specific title, genre of book.

Step 2. We match your keywords with Meta's Audience builder. This step puts your ad in front of those most likely to click on your ad. Rather than blasting it out to a million people who have no interest in your book.

Step 3. Write three test ads.

Step 4. Do simple $10. beta test for each ad to see which of these three ads receives the best results. Based on the data, how many people clicked on the ad, and how many bought the book, we can tell if you will make a profit from an ad campaign for that title.

Step 5. If the answer is no. We can write three more test ads with different keywords and run the test again. Or accept the results of the first test and conclude there's not enough interest in this title to make a profit.

Step 6. If the data shows an ad campaign will be profitable then it is up to you to decide what your ad budget is. This can be any number. But, we like to recommend one more test before a client jumps in with a big investment. Do a $100 campaign and verify that the results are duplicated before betting the farm.

These basic steps are the same used by professional ad agencies charging thousands of dollars per hour. To ignore these steps is, as I stated earlier: flushing $ down the toilet.

You receive all the analytics, graphs, charts etc. generated by Meta from all the test. So it's not us just making up stuff.

Our fee for steps one through four is: $129. The process takes about four to six days depending on wait times for the test results from meta. We like to do one test each on Mon, Wed, and

Fri, the busiest days for online shopping. It's a reasonable price to find out how many people are interested in your book.

WHAT THE HECK ARE Marketing Analytics?
After running a digital ad campaign, This data tell us:
A. how many people saw your ad, usually tens of thousands per test. If they were on a phone or laptop
B. How many clicked on it and when.
C. How many clicked on the link to your website, Amazon pg or your book page on Cadmus. (only one Link per ad)
D. If you use the Cadmus link: we have both, website analytics and Meta tracking on our site so we can tell how long the visitors stayed on your pg, if they buy and what link brought them to the site. Ie., was it a random person looking at Cadmus or was it a person who clicked on your ad.   Also what city, state, etc.

FAQs FOR AUTHORS COPIES and TAX LAW.
Does Cadmus charge me to order Authors copies? It depends. If you order less than ten copies there is a $8 admin fee. If you order 11 or more there is no charge.

Can I order Wholesale from Cadmus Publishing? (note: ordering wholesale implies not paying taxes on the order, that you will sell books, collect applicable taxes, or use the books as a promotional give away and not be libel for taxes)

To place wholesale orders, you, your company or representative must have a Tax license. Called a user tax license or Resale license.

What happens if I don't have a tax license?
You may still order at the discounted wholesale prices but must pay tax on the order. You may or may not add this amount to the price of your book and not report it to the state because the tax has been paid and documented.

Q: Does Cadmus take care of snail mail orders? A: Of course, what kind of publishing house that works with convicts would we be if we didn't deal in snail mail or snail mail orders?

SELL YOUR BOOKS FROM PRISON

Q: How many books do I have to buy when I publish?

A: Absolutely none player. Zero, zip, nada. (See the print on demand question)

Q: How do I know what the price of my book should be?

A: You got multiple options, its kind of a sliding scale. You can go the low ball route and price it as cheap as possible so that more people will buy it. Or you can go the high ball route and price it above average so as to entice people into thinking its more special than the others in its genre. Or you can start at a low price, build up buzz and sales, then switch to a higher price. Cadmus works with you to figure out the best price balanced with your desire for royalties.

Q: Does the title really matter. Hows that saying go, never judge a book by its title, right?

A: Its never judge a book by its cover, but essentially the same thing. Its also essentially bullshit. Yes, absolutely the title really matters. Think about nicknames. Would you wanna deal with a cat named "Rodent", or "Ratfink"? I think not. What if Mountain Dew was really called "Warm Piss", would you still drink it? Think about it like this, how many times have you yourself been scanning through an Edward R Hamilton or any other catalog and skipped over a potentially great book because the title and cover didn't jive with you, didn't peak your interest? It happened to me with a book titled Shantaram, I thought it was gonna be something real dumb, I didn't even read the synopsis. But I was wrong, boy was I so wrong. I was wrong because after being nagged into reading it by a homeboy, that book became one of my favorites.

Q: What the hell is "proof copy" of a manuscript?

A: A proof copy is created after you send us your manuscript, we sprinkle our magical fairy dust on it then wave our magic wand over it. Afterwards, what we send back for you to go through and give your thumbs up on, and to be published into the actual book, that is a proof copy of a manuscript.

Q: What's the difference between a web page and a website?

A: The internet says a web page is a single document on the web using a unique URL, while a website is a a collection of web pages in which information on a related topic is linked together under one domain address, like a dot com. For example, your author web page(s) on the Cadmus website will contain all your Cadmus published material and other optional features you may chose. Like selling merch with the title of your book. A website is generally not recommended unless you have the funds to bring traffic to to it.

Q: What are bindings?

A: Binding is the method used to hold a paperback or hard copy of a book together, not what the pigs put on your wrists when you've scared them. Workbooks can be spiral bound. The majority of books will be done in whats called the "perfect bound" method. This is the technical name for the binding on all trade paperbacks... the pages clamped together, then roughened along the spine hot glue is then forced a tiny distance up between the pages, holding em together. Then the cover is glued and wrapped around the spine.

Q: Does it make any difference what size my book is?

A: Yes, each genre of book has it's own size. Our layout department will automatically size your book to the correct genre.

Q: Does Cadmus supply names of people who buy my book?

A: Our distributors, Ingram and Amazon do not share customers data.

Q: I want my book on the shelves of every bookstore in the country. Does Cadmus make this happen?

A: That dog don't walk player. Check the math on this having 5 copies in one of every 20,000+ bookstores entails printing 100,000 copies at like $3.00 each. Do you he $300,000? plus another $500,000+ for shipping and some advertising/promotion? Also consider distributors and bookstores largely operate on a "returnable" basis, so you wouldn't see ANY income for about a year, and then you might get all 300,000 copies back. Like I said, that dog don't walk player.

Q: Can I revise my book after I get feedback from readers?

A: With on-demand publishing, its a piece of cake to make revisions to produce a new edition. At any point, you can send us replacement pages and we can swap them for the obsolete pages. We then send you another "proof" copy for you to once again give your thumbs up to publish.

GEORGE R. KAYER AND VINNIE VALE

PUBLICATIONS WHO PUBLISH PRISONERS

-THE ABOLITIONIST-
+ Critical Resistance
1904 Franklin St. She. 504
Oakland, CA 95612
+Info: This is a national organization with local chapters that fights prison expansion and supports abolishing prison entirely. They produce a newsletter for all people, but free specifically to prisoners.

-THE AMERICAN DISSIDENT-
+ American Dissident
217 Commerce Rd.
Barnstable, MA 02630
+Info: A national publication focusing on the experience, conflict, and/or involvement with "power". They also accept poems stemming from such experience.

-ART OF PRISON SURVIVAL-
+ (202) 383-1511
+ www.SafeStreetArts.info
+ Prison Foundation
2512 Virginia Ave, NW
#58043
Washington, DC 20037
+ A national bimonthly publication that profiles prison artists, as well as news of prisoners, activists, and programs that improve prison environments.

-BEYOND TODAY-
+ (513) 576-9796
+ www.BTMagazine.org
+Beyond Today
P.O. Box 54179
Cincinnati, OH 45254-0179
+ A national bimonthly Christian publication covering world trends and events, as well as family and social issues.

SELL YOUR BOOKS FROM PRISON

-COMPASSION-
+ Compassion
140 W. Boundary St.
Perrysburg, OH 43551
+ A national newsletter written by death row convicts.

-DAMIEN CENTER NEWSLETTER-
+ (317) 632-0123
+ Damien Center
26 N. Arsenal
Indianapolis, IN 46205
+ A national bimonthly newsletter covering AIDS related issues.

-DISCERN-
+ (972) 521-7777
+ www.LifeHopeAndTruth.com
+ Info@DiscernMag.com
+ Discern
P.O. Box 3409
McKinney, TX 75070
+ A national bimonthly Christian magazine covering commentary, world news, Christian living, and Biblical application.

-FIRE INSIDE-
+ Fire Inside
1540 Market St. #490
San Francisco, CA 94102
+ A national quarterly newsletter covering women's prisons.

-FREEDOM INSIDE-
+ www.FreedomInside.com
+ Freedom_Inside@HotMail.com
+ A national Christian newsletter designed for and written by convicts.

-FORTUNE NEWS-
+ Fortune Society

29-27 Northern Blvd.
Long Island City, NY 11101
+ Reports on prison conditions and criminal justice issues. Released quarterly.

-INCARCERATED VOICES-
+ www.IncarceratedVoices.com
+ A national newsletter and a website where convicts can speak out about their experiences in prison and give the general public info about our circumstances and conditions through our eyes.

-JUSTICE DENIED MAGAZINE-
+ (206) 335-4254
+ www.JusticeDenied.org
+ Contact@JusticeDenied.org
+ Justice Denied Magazine
P.O. Box 66291
Seattle, WA 98166
+ A national magazine that prints stories written by prisoners of wrongful conviction.

-MAOIST PRISON CELL-
+ www.PrisonCensorship.info
+ Maoist Prison Cell
P.O. Box 40799
San Francisco, CA 94140
+ A national newsletter promoting the anti-imperialist prison movment.

-THE MARSHALL PROJECT-
+ (212) 803-5200
+ www.TheMarshallProject.org
+ Info@TheMarshallProject.org
+ The Marshall Project
156 West 56th St., Suite 701
New York, NY 10019
+ A national news organization started by the former editor of The New York Times that publishes stories from prisoners on

SELL YOUR BOOKS FROM PRISON

their website.

-OFF OUR BACKS: A WOMEN'S NEWS JOURNAL-
+ (202) 234-8072
+ www.OffOurBacks.org
+ OffOurBacks@cs.org
+ Off Our Backs
2337B 18th St. NW
Washington, DC 20009
+ A national bimonthly journal that covers feminist issues/activism.

-THE PHILADELPHIA TRUMPET-
+ (800) 772-8577
+ www.TheTrumpet.com
+ The Trumpet
P.O. Box 3700
Edmond, OK 73083-3700
+ An international monthly Christian magazine.

-PRISON LEGAL NEWS-
+ www.PrisonLegalNews.com
+ Info@PrisonLegalNews.org
+ Prison Legal News
P.O. Box 1151
Lake Worth, FL 33460
+ An international and independent monthly publication that reports, reviews, and analyzes court rulings and news related to prisoners rights and prison issues.

-REACHING OUT-
+ NA World Services, Inc
P.O. Box 9999
Van Buys, CA 91409
+ A national newsletter published quarterly by Narcotics Anonymous covering addiction issues.

-SAN QUENTIN NEWS-
+ CSP- San Quentin

Education Dept./5Q News
San Quentin, Can 94964
+ A national publication edited and produced by convicts locked up in The Q.

-SINISTER WISDOM INC.-
+ (813) 502-5549
+ Sinister Wisdom
2333 McIntosh Road
Dover, FL 33527
+ A national literary journal covering Lesbian issues.

-SOLITARY WATCH-
+ www.SolitaryWatch.com
+ SolitaryWatchNews@Gmail.com
+ Solitary Watch
P.O. Box 11374
Washington, DC 20008
+ A newsletter that covers information and news about the conditions of solitary confinement.

-THE SUN MAGAZINE-
+ (919) 942-5282
+ www.TheSunMagazine.org
+ Editorial Office
107 North Roberson St.
Chapel Hill, NC 27516
+ A national independent monthly magazine that publishes personal essays, short stories, interviews, and poetry.

-SWORD OF THE LORD-
+ (800) 247-9673
+ www.SwordOfTheLord.com
+ Sword Of The Lord
P.O. Box 1099
Murfreeboro, TN 37133
+ A national bimonthly Christian newspaper that also offers a catalog of around 1,500 Christian books, and Bibles.

SELL YOUR BOOKS FROM PRISON

-TURNING THE TIDE-
+ Anti-Racist Action
P.O. Box 1055
Culver City, CA 90232
+ A national newspaper that covers the fight against racism.

GEORGE R. KAYER AND VINNIE VALE

FOR YOUR NOTES

SELL YOUR BOOKS FROM PRISON

FOR YOUR NOTES

FOR YOUR NOTES

SELL YOUR BOOKS FROM PRISON

FOR YOUR NOTES

FOR YOUR NOTES

SELL YOUR BOOKS FROM PRISON

FOR YOUR NOTES

GEORGE R. KAYER AND VINNIE VALE

FOR YOUR NOTES

SELL YOUR BOOKS FROM PRISON

FOR YOUR NOTES

FOR YOUR NOTES

SELL YOUR BOOKS FROM PRISON

FOR YOUR NOTES

GEORGE R. KAYER AND VINNIE VALE

www.ingramcontent.com/pod-product-compliance
Lightning Source LLC
Chambersburg PA
CBHW052144070526
44585CB00017B/1973